WRITING GOTHIC FICTION

by Rayne Hall

WRITING GOTHIC FICTION

by Rayne Hall

Book cover by Erica Syverson and Manuel Berbin

September 2019 Edition

ISBN: 9781688875913

Imprint: Independently published

British English

TABLE OF CONTENTS

INTRODUCTION

Romantic and creepy, passionate and thrilling, Gothic Fiction grabs readers and makes their hearts pound with excited suspense.

This is the genre of dark secrets, forbidden loves and illicit passions, of ancient curses and evil crimes. Brooding heroes, wealthy eccentrics, obsessed scientists and corrupt priests come to life in these tales, often joined by a ghost, werewolf, vampire or supernatural hound.

Stories are set in gloomy old houses and spooky mansions. Picture wild, windswept landscapes, sombre clouds and torrential rain. Stolen jewels, vile murders, an unexpected inheritance, bigamy, madness, illicit love and dangerous inventions all keep the readers glued to the pages.

Gothic is one of the oldest fiction genres, with classic masterpieces like *Wuthering Heights, Jane Eyre, Frankenstein, Dracula, Rebecca* and *The Fall of the House of Usher*. In the 21st century, they are represented by many Thrillers and Romance novels on current bestseller lists.

Few novels are undiluted Gothic. The most successful works of literature blend Gothic with other genres, the Gothic elements ratcheting up tension and enveloping the reader in suspense.

So you want to try your hand at writing a Gothic story? Maybe you have a draft novel in another genre that needs more passion and thrills? I'll be your guide, showing you step-by-step how to craft a Gothic tale.

You can use this book as a study course to learn the art of writing Gothic Fiction. I suggest you read the whole book, taking notes of the points that strike you and jotting down creative ideas as they come. Then return to the chapters you want to study in depth as you work on your own Gothic creation.

Use my suggestions as guidelines and prompts. They're not intended as rules, because every author's voice and every work of fiction is unique. Choose which tropes you want to develop and which tips you want to apply, then adapt them to suit your vision and style.

This book is for experienced writers who want to add to their toolkit. If you're new to the craft of fiction writing, you can still enjoy this book and pick up useful techniques, but writers who've already mastered the basics of their craft will benefit the most.

I'm writing in British English. If you're used to American English, some word choices, spellings, grammatical constructions and punctuation placements may look odd... but I'm sure you'll be able to follow me. For simplicity, I'll use the female pronoun 'she' when referring to the main character, because it's less clunky than 'he or she' and because most Gothic Fiction features a woman as the protagonist. Feel free to write about a man instead. Gender roles are not gender rules.

Are you ready to delve into the mystery and excitement of the Gothic tale? Let's open the portal to the old mansion. Can you hear the hinges squeal? Duck under the cobwebs, and mind that trap door under your feet. Take a few steps on the threadbare crimson carpet while I light a candle to show you the way.

Rayne Hall

CHAPTER 1

UNDERSTANDING THE GENRE

Rich in action, emotion and suspense, Gothic stories keep readers on the edge of their chair with excitement. Gloomy old houses, brooding heroes, windswept landscapes, villains, vampires and ghosts reveal the secrets of their forbidden passions. Gothic Fiction resonates deep in the readers' subconscious with dark twists and intense emotions.

Some systems class Gothic as a genre of its own, others treat it as a sub-genre of Horror. Most often, Gothic overlaps with other genres. You'll find Gothic Thrillers, Gothic Romance, Gothic Fantasy, Literary Gothic and more – and in these blends, Gothic is most original and compelling. I've read many novels that straddle two or more genres including Gothic – and an astonishing number of them are famous classics and recent top bestsellers.

Adding Gothic elements to a work of genre fiction is like adding another layer, similar to the way a chef might add a new ingredient to a familiar dish to heighten the flavour and delight the diner's taste buds.

Whatever genre you normally write, Gothic is a harmonious fit. Go ahead and layer Gothic with Western, Urban Fantasy, Regency Romance, Cosy Mystery, Christian Inspirational, M2M Erotica, Steampunk, Satire, Middle Grade, YA Paranormal... the opportunities are endless. Gothic provides suspense, romance, dark twists, thrills and plot elements that resonate in the reader's subconscious.

I suggest you combine Gothic with the genre you normally write (or plan to write), so you're not leaving your niche, but adding a new facet to your body of work and enriching your brand. In the chapter 'Mix and Match: Layering Genres' I'll provide some tips for this.

Of course, you can also write stories that are pure Gothic.

Lovers of Gothic Fiction divide the genre into several subcategories, for example by period (Victorian Gothic, Contemporary Gothic) and by region (Russian Gothic, Southern Ontario Gothic).

However, these classifications are not strict. In modern publishing, the boundaries between different genres and subgenres tend to blur, and in the case of Gothic Fiction, they are especially fluid.

FAMOUS WORKS OF GOTHIC FICTION

Here are some great works of literature you may have read or heard of. All of these are distinctly Gothic – but most belong to one or several other genres as well.

Edgar Allan Poe: *The Fall of the House of Usher*

Stephen King: *The Shining*

Arthur Conan Doyle: *The Hound of the Baskervilles*

Wilkie Collins: *The Woman in White*

William Faulkner: *Sanctuary*

Mary Stewart: *The Gabriel Hounds*

Angela Carter: *The Lady of the House of Love*

Daphne du Maurier: *Rebecca*

Emily Bronte: *Wuthering Heights*

Charlotte Bronte: *Jane Eyre*

Bram Stoker: *Dracula*

Mary Shelley: *Frankenstein*

Shirley Jackson: *The Haunting of Hill House*

Georgette Heyer: *Cousin Kate*

Diane Setterfield: *The Thirteenth Tale*

Elizabeth Kostova, *The Historian*

Audrey Niffenegger: *The Adventuress*

Margaret Atwood: *The Blind Assassin*

Truman Capote: *Other Voices, Other Rooms*

Robin McKinley: *Sunshine*

Ann Rice: *Interview with the Vampire*

Amanda DeWees, *Nocturne for a Widow*

Robert Louis Stevenson: *The Strange Case of Dr Jekyll and Mr Hyde*

The first Gothic novel was *The Castle of Otranto* by Horace Walpole.

WHERE DOES THE WORD 'GOTHIC' COME FROM?

Gothic originally meant something of the Goths, an ancient Germanic tribe who played a role in the fall of the Roman Empire. Later, the word came to stand for medieval art, architecture and culture. Since some of the earliest Gothic novels, penned in the 18th century, were set in the Middle Ages, readers described them as 'Gothic'.

Today's Gothic Fiction is rarely related to either the ancient Gothic tribe or mediaeval culture, but the term persists.

'Gothic' is also used to describe a clothing style (with red, black and purple as the dominant colours, and medieval or Victorian designs), a style of architecture (with rib-vaulted ceilings, flying buttresses and pointed arches) and a style of music (dark rock with romantic lyrics). In this guide, we'll look at the Gothic literary style.

ASSIGNMENTS

1. Do you plan to write a pure Gothic story? Or do you want to blend Gothic with another genre you enjoy reading or have experience writing – and if yes, which?

2. Pick one or several works of Gothic Fiction from the list that you haven't read yet, and study them. Many are classics out of copyright, and you'll be able to find them free online. With others, you can download and read the free sample chapters to discover what they're like and if they suit your taste. You may discover a new favourite author, deepen your understanding of the genre, and gain inspiration for your own writing.

CHAPTER 2

THE TROPES OF GOTHIC FICTION

'Tropes' are recurring motifs in literary works, and Gothic Fiction is rich in them. The Gothic tropes work on the readers' subconscious to stir emotions.

I've compiled a list, loosely grouped by context. As you read the list, highlight the ones that appeal to you. You don't need to use them all – simply pick the ones that intrigue and inspire you. Interpret them creatively, mix them with other plot elements and develop them in your personal style, ensuring your story is original, exciting and fresh.

THEMES AND ISSUES

Choosing one or several of these will give your novel meaning and depth. In the chapter 'How to Convey your Novel's Message' we'll look at how to write about how to weave these issues into your fiction plot.

Justice/injustice

Power/powerlessness

Wealth/poverty

Class conflicts (e.g. master/servant, slavery)

Gender issues (e.g. the status of women in society, feminism, legal injustices)

Marginalisation

Mental illness

Loyalty/betrayal

Vengeance

Degeneration and decay (of people, buildings, objects, morals)

SETTING

The settings are hugely important in Gothic Fiction. For my own stories, I often start with an idea for a location, and then develop the story from there. Pick several items from this list. You'll find that they combine well. In later chapters, I'll give you specific tips for using some of these locations for the greatest literary effects.

An old gloomy building – often in a state of decay

An underground room (storage cellar, dungeon, torture chamber, secret passage, crypt, cave)

An attic

A secret passage

Isolated location – some distance from the nearest settlement

Wild, exciting natural landscape

Foreign travel

Exotic location

A grand staircase

A religious building (convent, monastery, temple, chapel)

Strong wind (storm, gale, blizzard, thunderstorm)

Unseasonal/freak weather (e.g. snow in summer, torrential rain after a drought)

Midnight

Twilight (dawn, dusk)

A cemetery (graveyard, mausoleum, burial ground, unmarked grave)

A cavern, cave or tunnel

CHARACTERS

In Gothic Fiction, characters often have strong archetypal qualities as well as individual features. In the chapters 'The Main Character: Newcomer in Jeopardy' and 'Meet the Cast: Recurring Characters' I'll guide you how to develop them. For now, just choose the kind of people you want to write about.

A naive bride

A scientist or inventor

A brooding anti-hero

A power-crazed or greedy villain

A loyal servant

A dog (pet, best friend, guard dog, monster, laboratory animal)

A ghost

A vampire

A corrupt religious professional (priest, rabbi, shaman, nun, monk)

A corrupt doctor/healer

An invalid (an elderly, frail or sickly character)

A corrupt guardian (of a child, of a property, of nature)

An abuser who turned to evil after he was abused himself

A sinner who has repented and seeks redemption for the evil of his past

DEATH AND THE OCCULT

With or without paranormal elements, death plays a role in almost all Gothic Fiction. You can play up or tone down the paranormal aspects as you wish. Depending on the type of story you write, you can use them as part of the main plot, or simply mention them as a local superstition practised by a minor character.

A grave (cemetery, mausoleum, skeleton of bricked-up-alive victim)

Communicating with the dead (e.g. spiritualism, seances, ouija board)

Ghosts, zombies, vampires, other undead

Time travel

A curse

A dark prophecy

A portal between the past and the present

A dying character

DARK SECRETS

Secrets are a must in Gothic Fiction – preferably dark, guilty ones. Pick one or several that intrigue you. In the chapter 'Guilty Secrets, Secret Guilt' I'll show you how to weave them into the plot.

Bigamy (current, or in past generations, or about to be attempted)

Sexual deviation

A secret prisoner

A falsified or hidden last will and testament

A secret identity (someone is not who he seems to be)

A secret scientific discovery or invention

Illegal drugs (addiction, trade, smuggling)

A secret passage or room

A secret going back several generations

A falsified ancestral line

Incest

Kidnapping

Human trafficking

A terrible crime (committed in the past, ongoing in the present, planned in the future)

EMOTIONS

Gothic Fiction is intensely emotional. Make your readers feel what your characters do. In the chapters 'Driving Passions and Obsessions', 'Trust No One: Resentment and Betrayal' and 'Viscerals: Stir up the Reader's Emotions' I'll delve deeply into this topic and show you techniques to arouse the reader's emotions.

Obsession

Passion (smouldering, forbidden, mad)

Love – true

Love – unrequited

Love – obsessive

Love – thwarted

Love – doomed

Love – undying (literally undying… continuing beyond death)

Lust (often with obsessive desires)

Deviant sexual needs (including shocking perversions)

Fear (apprehension, suspense, dread, horror, terror)

OBJECTS

Pick one or several items that intrigue you personally.

A work of art (often a painting)

An old book (often very old)

A last will and testament

A journal (of an ancestor, a long-dead person, or a currently missing person)

A long-lost re-discovered document (treasure map, will, confession)

A piece of jewellery (often very old, inherited from an ancestor)

A chest (any size – from a tiny jewellery box to a steamer trunk to a sarcophagus, often from another part of the world and very old)

OTHER

These combine well with the other motifs, so add them liberally.

A broken promise/vow

A vow kept at enormous costs

A terrible beast

The colour red (blood red, scarlet, crimson, wine red, purple)

The number 13

Drugs (prescription, illegal, smuggled, madness-inducing)

An escape

Ancestors

Disaster (inferno, flood, earthquake, tsunami)

Sacrifice (a ritual sacrifice, or a character gives up something out of loyalty to someone else)

Modern technology (or former state-of-the-art technology, now out-of-date)

Modern science with scientific experiments

WHAT NOT TO DO

Don't write a story consisting of nothing but tropes. The result would feel clichéd. Make sure you mix the tropes with other elements.

ASSIGNMENTS

1. Think of a Gothic novel you've read, or read one now. Identify the Gothic tropes in this work. You may be surprised how many of the tropes it contains.

2. Highlight all the tropes that intrigue you. You will use those (or at least, some of them) in your story.

CHAPTER 3

THE GLOOMY OLD HOUSE: ENTER THE LAIR OF SECRETS

In Gothic Fiction, the story often involves a big, old, dark, decayed house. This building plays an important role in the plot and is practically a character in its own right. So let's create the Gloomy House.

Typically, it's a castle or manor house – but it could also be a tower, a hotel, a farm, a factory, a sanatorium, a hospital, a skyscraper, a school, a lighthouse, a prison, a mental health care facility, an airport terminal, a lighthouse, a theatre, a monastery, a beach hut…. Just make sure it has a history.

For literary inspiration, here are some famous Gloomy Houses from literature:

Wuthering Heights in Emily Bronte's *Wuthering Heights*

Hill House in Shirley Jackson's *The Haunting of Hill House*

Furnivall Manor in Elizabeth Gaskell's *The Old Nurse's Story*

The Overlook Hotel in Stephen King's *The Shining*

Manderley in Daphne du Maurier's *Rebecca*

Staplewood in Georgette Heyer's *Cousin Kate*

Dar Ibrahim in Mary Stewart's *The Gabriel Hounds*

Chateau de Valmy in Mary Stewart's *Nine Coaches Waiting*

Sometimes, a vehicle – old, dilapidated and creepy – takes the role of the Gloomy House. Example from literature: the haunted coach in *The Phantom Coach* by Amelia Edwards. At the end of this book, I've included my Gothic story *The Train to Dolno Orehovo* in which events unfold on a train.

LOCATION

If possible, place the house some distance away from the nearest settlements. This aids plotting, because the Main Character in jeopardy can't easily call on neighbours to get help. The building could be a remote castle, a hotel on an island or a chalet in the Alps. Even if the Gloomy House stands in a city, aim to surround it with bombed-out ruins or vast parks.

It helps if the Gloomy House stands in a wild, exciting location, surrounded by sublime nature, whether it's on the edge of a desert, on a windswept moor, on a steep mountain or a rocky seashore cliff – and if possible, choose a place where storms batter the land.

It also helps the plot if there is no mobile phone (cellphone) coverage.

Readers enjoy exotic locations, so they get to travel to exciting places at the cost of a paperback and from the safety of their armchair.

Bear in mind that what readers perceive as exotic and exciting may be everyday reality to you. If you've spent most of your life in a village in the Austrian Alps, the scenery and routines are so familiar that you think of them as boring and predictable. But to your readers elsewhere in the world, staying in a mountain village in Austria is thrilling and new.

If you place your Gloomy House in the region where you live, you'll need to spend little time on research, and your descriptions will ring with authenticity.

Alternatively, you can use your next holidays (vacations) to explore a new location for your Gothic Fiction.

DECAYED AND DILAPIDATED

Once an attractive residence, the Gloomy House is long past its glory days. Signs of decay abound – cracked walls, mouldy ceilings, leaking roofs, overgrown gardens.

The manor may be so dilapidated that only one wing is still habitable. The hospital may have had to close most of its departments after budget cuts. The office block may have only one floor still in use.

LAYOUT

The Gloomy House probably features one or several of the following:

- An underground chamber. (This can be a wine cellar, sauna, home gym, a guest apartment, basement kitchen, laboratory, boiler room, workshop, air raid shelter, underground chapel, dungeon or crypt.)

- An attic. (This could be a loft or a penthouse, servant's quarters or storage space for half-forgotten clutter.)

- A secret passage (Perhaps there's a narrow corridor leading from the master's bedroom to that of the governess, or an underground tunnel leading from the cellar to the church.)

- A hiding space (such as the 'priest hole' found in many old British buildings, or a bricked up haunted room)

- A grand staircase

- A high-tech feature (or a feature that was high-tech when it was built, but is now out-of-date)

- An ancestor gallery

USE A REAL HOUSE FOR INSPIRATION

If there's a big, old and perhaps decayed house in your neighbourhood, use it for inspiration. You can walk past there, maybe even go inside (if it's open to the public) and take detailed notes.

You could also set the story in a house similar to the one you grew up in, a hotel where you spent your Christmas holidays, or a remote scientific observation post where you used to work.

Don't use the real house as it is – certainly not with its real name and address. You don't want to get into trouble with its real owners who would probably not be happy to have their home showcased as a place of bigamy and murder. Use the house for inspiration, but change the name, the address, architectural details and features.

Also, adapt the house to suit the story. Make it bigger, older, gloomier, give it an underground chamber, a secret tunnel and a creaking staircase, or move it further away from its nearest neighbours.

EXAMPLES FROM LITERATURE

Wuthering Heights by Emily Bronte

Wuthering Heights is the name of Mr Heathcliff's dwelling. 'Wuthering' being a significant provincial adjective, descriptive of the atmospehric tumult to which its station is exposed in stormy weather. Pure, bracing ventilation they must have up there at all times, indeed: one may guess the power of the north wind blowing over the edge, by the excessive slant of a few stunted firs at the end of the house; and by a range of gaunt thorns all stretching their limbs one way, as if craving the alms of the sun. Happily, the architect had the foresight to build it strong: the narrow windows are deeply set in the wall, and the corners defended with large jutting stones.

Nocturne for a Widow, by Amanda DeWees

Brooke House was massive, built of great blocks of what I later learned was limestone; in the eerie radiance of twilight it was a pearlescent blue-grey like a stormy sky. Mullioned windows in arched stone casements were everywhere, including the gables, which were ornamented with lacy spires. Crenellations along the roof line added to the medieval effect. There was a square tower with more spires, as well as a round window reminiscent of a cathedral's rose window. Some of the windows were shuttered, but light glowed from behind the massive arched window next to the front door.

WHAT NOT TO DO

Don't use a bland, generic setting for your Gothic Fiction. Use the opportunity to invite your readers to a dramatic location.

ASSIGNMENT

1. Choose the building. Whether it exists in your neighbourhood, in your memories, in your imagination or in a combination of those, describe it. Write a few sentences about its architecture, layout, size, location, history. (Later, you can fine-tune the details to make them fit your story plot.)

2. Give your house either an underground room, an attic or a hidden chamber. Is it secret? Forgotten? Dangerous to get in? Or is it in use, and if yes, for what?

3. Visit a real-life building for inspiration. Choose one that's as similar to the Gloomy House of your inspiration. For example, if you've chosen to write about a hotel, go and have a coffee in the lobby of a nearby hotel, even if it's not decayed and gloomy). Go inside if that's possible, or just view the facade from the outside.

Take notes of small atmospheric details:

- What does the floor look like?

- And the ceiling?

- What's the source and quality of the light?

- How do doors sound when they open and close?

- What kind of vegetation surrounds it?

- If there are people, how do they talk, move, behave?

- Are there any signs of decay? (Signs of decay are fantastic for creating an ominous mood. Watch out for cracks in the facade, a path overgrown with weeds, a dead pot plant, broken windows, peeling paint.)

- Describe the windows from the outside.

- What smells are there? (Smells can be difficult to notice and identify, but it's worth trying: does a room smell of mildew, old urine, candle smoke, rotting fruit, rat droppings or moth balls?)

- Listen for noises, especially background sounds. The more sounds you collect, the better, because these will be very useful for creating suspense. Cutlery rattling, water gurgling in the pipes, a coffee maker hissing, footsteps clacking on the tiles, a cock crowing, a car motor whining...)

If you're unable to visit a suitable building, look at pictures or videos. (Maybe you have photos in an album or can find something on YouTube.) This won't yield the kind of atmospheric details you ideally want, but it's better than nothing.

CHAPTER 4

THE MAIN CHARACTER: NEWCOMER IN JEOPARDY

The main character (MC) is usually female (but can be male), is vulnerable because of her position as a newcomer, but possesses inner strength. She is an outsider who takes up residence in the Gloomy House.

In this book, I'm using the female pronoun for the MC, simply because the protagonists in Gothic Fiction are almost always women. However, feel free to set this convention aside and make your MC a man. My tips apply regardless of the gender.

WHY DOES SHE STAY IN THE GLOOMY HOUSE?

In what way is she an outsider, and why does she take up residence in this strange place? There are four main possibilities:

1. She has inherited the Gloomy House, probably because of an eccentric will.

2. Family circumstances force her to live there. Perhaps she's newly married to the owner of the Gloomy House, or perhaps she's recently orphaned or divorced, has lost her home and needs to live with unwelcoming relations in the Gloomy House.

3. She is only visiting the house or travelling in the vicinity, when calamity strikes (her car breaks down, her coach is attacked by highwaymen, a snowstorm forces her to seek shelter). She means to stay only for a night, but finds she can't get away again (because the snowstorm continues to rage, or because the owner is pleased to have a living soul as a companion, or

because the villain won't allow her to get away after she has seen clues to the Guilty Secret).

4. She's there on a job or assignment (probably a live-in job, or an assignment requiring her to stay in the guest bedroom for several nights). She could be, for example, a governess, a servant, a chef, the hotel's new receptionist, an interior designer, a musician, a maintenance engineer, a hired entertainer, a house minder, a pet-sitter, an au pair, an art restorer, a nurse, a nanny, a librarian, a historian, an antiques valuer, a furniture restorer, a painter and decorator, a journalist, a researcher for a documentary, a location scout for a movie company, an estate agent assessing the property or a paranormal investigator.

Option 4 gives probably the most scope for contemporary Gothic stories and is the one modern readers will find easiest to believe. It has the added advantage that it provides the MC with useful skills and insights which can drive the plot forward in plausible ways. For example, as the child's nanny or governess, she'll naturally observe that something is wrong with her charge. If she's a nurse, she'll notice clues pointing to the visiting doctor's malpractice. If she's an antiques valuer, it makes sense that she discovers the secret drawer in the old desk. As a painter and decorator, she'll spot the bricked-up door to the secret passage, and as a musician, she'll recognise the tune the ghostly violin plays at midnight.

STRONG YET VULNERABLE

She has some kind of inner strength: probably moral strength, loyalty and the courage of conviction. She may also have determination and willpower. Often, she possesses grit acquired during a tough childhood. You can give her other strengths to suit your story.

Her vulnerability stems mostly from her situation. She's a stranger, with no friends in the house or the neighbourhood (and perhaps no friends or family at all). She doesn't know the location and the customs, and perhaps not even the language.

Many people openly dislike her, and some resent her (perhaps because they expected to inherit the house, get the job or marry the man) or suspect her intentions.

In addition, the matter of class may separate her from other people who might otherwise like and trust her. The classic example is the governess, whom neither the family nor the servants regard as one of their own. She could also be a free black woman where others are slaves, a hired help where others are society ladies, or a commoner where others are gentry.

Her vulnerability may be further increased by lack of money. Whatever happened in the past has left her penniless (and possibly homeless, too). She may have been fired from her last job and has been jobhunting desperately for months, her savings depleted. She may have emerged destitute from an acrimonious divorce. Perhaps her father gambled away the family fortune and then shot himself. Maybe she was the victim of a robbery or scam. Perhaps her home in a war zone was bombed, and she was the only survivor, escaping with nothing but the clothes on her back.

Whatever the cause of her poverty, it means she desperately needs this job and/or this accommodation. That's why she doesn't leave at the first sign that something is wrong.

You could give her an additional problem to increase here vulnerability: shyness, anxiety, mental health issues, a physical disability, an inferiority complex, her own guilty secret….

As with all suggestions in this book, these are just guidelines, not rules. You can use the elements you like and discard anything you don't. I suggest that you make your main character 'Gothic' in the sense that several of these features apply to her, but you can choose which. And, importantly, make her more than just a Gothic prop. Flesh her out as a real character.

PROFESSIONAL TIP

Give the main character facets of your own personality and experience. For example, if you love dogs and fear heights, give the MC the same passion and fear. If you had a bewildering time as a new bride in your in-laws' home, dig deep into your memories of feelings and tensions. As a geriatric nurse, you can write believably about the nurse who cares for the invalid and spots the doctor's malpractice. If you have acting experience, you can give a new perspective on *Hamlet* by writing about a player hired to perform at Elsinore Castle. Do you collect antiques as a hobby? Then you can describe the furniture the way the antiques restorer MC sees it. Did you support yourself during your college days by cleaning hotel rooms? Then you can write with authenticity about the new chambermaid's work in the remote hotel.

ASSIGNMENT

1. Why does the main character go to live in the Gloomy House?

2. What is her job (if she has one)? What useful, potentially plot-relevant skills do her job and hobbies give her?

3. In what way is she vulnerable? (Choose at least one specific reason, several if possible.)

4. Jot down anything else about her that you know at this stage. (You're not committing to her profile at this stage. You can still make changes once you start plotting in earnest.)

CHAPTER 5

MEET THE CAST: RECURRING CHARACTERS

In Gothic Fiction, certain types show up again and again: the loyal retainer, the obsessed scientist, the corrupt doctor, the greedy villain, the sickly invalid, the helpless child, the naive bride, the old eccentric, the mentally deranged person….

What's interesting is that each character can assume several of these roles.

For example, the mentally deranged person may also be the helpless child – or he may be the greedy villain, or the obsessed scientist, or the old eccentric at the end of his life.

The newly arrived outsider could also be the naive bride or the sickly invalid or the obsessed scientist – or perhaps all of those.

This 'mix-and-match' ensures that the characters aren't cardboard copies repeated in every story.

(And of course, you'll need to create fully fleshed-out individual characters – but hopefully I won't need to teach you how to do that.) Another advantage of this 'mix-and-match' is that it keeps the cast list down to a manageable number.

So now let's look at these characters – or perhaps I should say, 'types' or even 'roles' because each character in your story may play more than one role. They all can be either male or female, whatever suits your tale. As you read through this list, consider which of them might fit your story. Then play around with combinations. Who might also be who?

THE NEWLY ARRIVED OUTSIDER

This is usually the MC we've looked at in the previous chapter. Sometimes, she's the Naive Bride, or she may be revealed to be the True Heir.

Examples from literature: In *Cousin Kate* by Georgette Heyer, the MC is a poor relation who needs a place to live. *Jane Eyre* by Charlotte Bronte and *Nine Coaches Waiting* by Mary Stewart both feature governesses starting out in a new job. The MC in *The Gabriel Hounds* by Mary Stewart visits the Gloomy House because she is curious to meet her eccentric relative.

THE GREEDY VILLAIN

Gothic villains are motivated by greed more than anything else. They may use cruelty and abuse their power to satisfy this greed. The Greedy Villain may be bitter because he himself has suffered great injustice, and perhaps he has devoted his life to revenge. If he's the Obsessed Scientist, he'll use his invention to get rich. If he's the Evil Charmer, he'll make his potential victim fall in love with him and convince everyone that he is innocent. Although evil, he may have a good and noble side to his character.

Examples from literature: In *Cousin Kate* by Georgette Heyer, Lady Broome, who sacrificed a lot to care for her sick husband, feels entitled to own the Gloomy House and will go to any lengths to keep it for herself and her descendants. In *The Gabriel Hounds* by Mary Stewart, the villains scheme to get Lady Harriet's wealth.

THE BIGAMIST

He's already married and wants to wed a new wife – either because he's obsessively in love with the girl or because she's an heiress and he wants her fortune. To achieve this, he denies his first wife's existence, hides her away (in the underground chamber or the attic), fakes evidence that the marriage wasn't valid (with the help of the Corrupt Priest) or poisons her (with the help of the Corrupt Doctor) so he'll be a widower and free to take a new wife. Alternatively, the bigamist is truly widowed, but his deceased wife continues to rule the Gloomy House as a ghost, either terrorising the new bride or warning her. Sometimes, the Bigamist and his wives are long dead, but their descendants survive, and when the bigamy comes to light, it changes the line of inheritance.

Examples from literature: In the earliest Gothic novel, *The Castle of Otranto* by Horace Walpole, Sir Manfred schemes to rid himself of his wife so he can marry a young princess. In Charlotte Bronte's novel *Jane Eyre*, Mr Rochester is the Bigamist. He loves the governess and wants to marry her, but already has a wife – a madwoman locked in the attic.

THE LOYAL RETAINER

This faithful servant may be the housekeeper, the butler, the secretary or the lady's maid. She has worked in this household for years or decades, perhaps since the days when the current master was a baby. Perhaps her parents and grandparents served the same family. The loyal retainer probably knows the Guilty Secret and may even be part of it. She's very loyal to her master…. But there may be a twist: to which master? For example, her true master may be the immortal vampire living in the crypt below the Gloomy House. The Loyal Retainer may at the same time be the Corrupt Doctor, or the Ghost, or the Dog.

Examples from literature: In Daphne du Maurier's novel *Rebecca*, the Loyal Retainer is the housekeeper Mrs Danvers, and she is loyal to the master's deceased first wife. In *The Old Nurse's Story* by Elizabeth Gaskell, the nurse narrator is loyal first to the young couple who employ her, and then to their orphaned child.

THE OBSESSED SCIENTIST

A scientist, alchemist or inventor, either an amateur or a professional, experiments with the latest technology or scientific formulas. His inventions may be benign (seeking a cure for cancer) or evil (developing a weapon of mass destruction). He is so obsessed with his experiments that he ruins his physical or mental health (making him the Sickly Invalid or the Mentally Deranged Person). He could be devoted to curing the sickly invalid, or he could carry out human experiments on the Captive, the Helpless Child or the Mentally Deranged Person. Sometimes he's the Loyal Retainer or the Corrupt Doctor. If you layer Science Fiction or Steampunk with Gothic, the Obsessed Scientist and his work may be at the centre of the plot.

Examples from literature: In Mary Shelly's novel *Frankenstein*, the MC Victor Frankenstein is obsessed with creating a new person from the body parts of dead people. In *Dr Jekyll and Mr Hyde* by Robert Louis Stevenson, Dr Jekyll is a respected scientist who meddles with the dark side of science to create his alter ego, and can't stop, even when he realises the evil nature of Mr Hyde.

THE CORRUPT DOCTOR

This can be a medical doctor, a nurse, a physiotherapist, a naturopath, a masseur or someone else with a healing role. Charged with caring for a patient who lives in the Gloomy House (the Sickly Invalid, the Mentally Deranged Person, the Helpless Child or the Old Eccentric), the Corrupt Doctor deliberately makes the illness worse instead of better. He may be in the pay of the Greedy Villain, or he may pursue his own interests. He may drive his victim to insanity (so nobody will believe her when she reveals the sinister goings on), poison her slowly, keep her bedridden (so she can't reveal the secret) or murder her (so someone else will inherit her wealth).

Examples from literature: In Georgette Heyer's *Cousin Kate,* Dr Delabole helps to hide the criminal insanity of the young heir. In

The Gabriel Hounds by Mary Stewart, Dr Henry Grafton schemes to get his share of Lady Harriet's wealth.

THE SICKLY INVALID

This person needs constant care, and never leaves the Gloomy House. She may be suffering with the patience of an angel, or she may be a cranky demanding patient. Often, the Corrupt Doctor is in charge of caring for her. Sometimes, the Sickly Invalid is also the Helpless Child, but she could also be the Old Eccentric, the Naive Bride, the True Heir, the Captive or the Mentally Deranged Person.

Examples from literature: In *The Toll-Gate* by Georgette Heyer, bedridden Sir Peter knows he's about to die and has many regrets – but on his deathbed, he manages to pull off a scheme that will protect his granddaughter from the villains' machinations. In *The Old Nurse's Story* by Elizabeth Gaskell, Miss Furnivall is a wrinkled, nearly deaf octogenarian with a Guilty Secret from the days of her youth.

THE CORRUPT PRIEST

A religious professional (priest, monk, nun, shaman, rabbi, swami, meditation retreat leader…) inspires trust because of his role, and he abuses this position. As a Catholic priest, he betrays a secret he's heard in confession. As a cult leader, he stirs up religious fervour to drive people to commit crimes in the name of faith. As a monk, he solicits donations for a charitable cause and keeps the funds for himself.

Examples from literature: In *The Monk* by Matthew Gregory Lewis, the viciously cruel Prioress Mother St Agatha keeps a girl prisoner in the dungeons beneath the convent and spreads the word about her death. In Thomas M. Disch's novel *The Priest,* Father Patrick Bryce is a Catholic priest with a paedophile past.

THE HELPLESS CHILD

The Helpless Child may be a baby, a toddler or a teenager, but is definitely a minor in the eyes of the law. Who cares for her? Who is her legal representative? She may be in the power of the Abusive Guardian. The child is often the Sickly Invalid and/or the True Heir. If she's the heir, then her fortune maybe administered by the Abusive Guardian, too. The Helpless Child is often a personification of angelic innocence, however, in some stories, she's evil. She may also be innocent, but becomes possessed by an evil spirit that drives her to commit cruelties.

Examples from literature: In *The Old Nurse's Story* by Elizabeth Gaskell, young Rosamond follows the ghost of a pretty little girl out into the cold and is found nearly frozen to death. In *Nine Coaches Waiting*, Philippe de Valmy is a lonely nine-year-old boy, owner of the opulent Château de Valmy and the title Comte de Valmy, but powerless in the hands of his guardians.

THE ABUSIVE GUARDIAN

The Abusive Guardian has charge of the Helpless Child – perhaps he's simply an employed tutor paid to teach the child for a few hours every day, or perhaps he is her guardian in the legal sense, a quasi-parent who administers her fortune and makes decisions. He may scheme that she will not survive to reach adulthood (so he himself will inherit her wealth), or plan to marry her to his son, or to marry her himself to get his hands on her fortune. He will keep her isolated, perhaps on the grounds of her alleged ill health (in which case she's also the Sickly Invalid or the Mentally Deranged Person), and instead of allowing her to go to school, he has her home-schooled.

Examples from literature: In *Cousin Kate* by Georgette Heyer, Lady Broome keeps her mentally ill son isolated, scheming to get him married at a young age so he will father a legal heir. In *Nine Coaches Waiting*, cynical disabled Léon de Valmy is not only the guardian of his nine-year-old nephew, but also the trustee of the boy's property.

THE NAIVE BRIDE

Shy, inexperienced in the ways of the world, poor, socially inept, without family or friends, the Naive Bride has fallen in love with the man who owns the Gloomy Place and moves in. He may turn out to be the Greedy Villain, the Obsessed Scientist, the Evil Charmer or the Mentally Deranged Person, and she may find herself the Captive and perhaps destined to become the Mentally Deranged Person. She may also discover that she has married the Bigamist.

Examples from literature: In Daphne du Maurier's novel *Rebecca*, the unnamed narrator marries a widower and naively assumes they'll live happily ever after – but then discovers that his late wife Rebecca rules over their lives. In *The Woman in White* by Wilkie Collins, the orphaned heiress Laura Fairlie, guileless and gentle, finds that the man she's fallen in love with and married wants her fortune and plots her death.

THE CAPTIVE

This person is in the power of the Evil Villain or the Obsessed Scientist. Maybe she's recently arrived, stumbled upon the Guilty Secret, and therefore is not allowed to leave again. Or maybe she's been imprisoned all her life, or her existence is inconvenient to someone. She's probably locked into the underground chamber or the attic.

Examples from literature: In *The Woman in White* by Wilkie Collins, MC Laura is kept captive by her husband – at first at home, and then under a false identity in a lunatic asylum. In *Jane Eyre* by Charlotte Bronte, the mentally ill Bertha Mason is kept locked up in the attic.

THE OLD ECCENTRIC

Nearing the end of his life, the Old Eccentric is probably rich – but he might also have lost his fortune long ago, or maybe people merely suspect that he has riches hidden away. Sometimes the Old Eccentric has already died, and people search for his last will and testament, or they argue over whether the will is valid since the Old Eccentric was obviously a Mentally Deranged Person. Maybe the Old Eccentric died generations ago, and now he haunts the Gloomy House. Either way, the Old Eccentric's last will and testament probably plays a role in the plot.

Example from literature: In *The Gabriel Hounds* by Mary Stewart, old Aunt Harriet chooses to live in the decaying splendour of an old palace near Beirut, dressed in male Arab garb, and changes her will every six months.

THE INSIDE CONFIDANT

This is a servant/fellow employee living in the Gloomy House whom the MC trusts. However, the Inside Confidant is powerless, and can't do more much more than warn the MC of specific dangers. The Inside Confidant can be a servant who depends on her job and can't take risks, or she may be a fellow victim and is often brainwashed. It's not entirely sure how trustworthy she really is. She may truly want to help the MC, but the master of the house has such power over her that she may cave in and betray the MC out of fear.

Example from literature: In *Cousin Kate* by Georgette Heyer, the MC's maid is friendly and supportive, but is herself powerless.

THE MENTALLY DERANGED PERSON

Any kind of madness or mental instability works here. The character may simply get occasional bouts of paranoia, or she may have lingering PTSD and be otherwise sane. Perhaps she never got over the grief at the death of her child. Maybe she suffers from schizophrenia. She could be a raving lunatic or a criminally insane serial killer. Perhaps incest practised over generations has led to inbreeding and mental weakness. Perhaps she lives voluntarily in the Gloomy House, hoping that the quiet location will aid her recovery. Or perhaps her relatives keep her hidden here (probably in the underground chamber or the attic) because she would be an embarrassment in society. Maybe the Obsessed Scientist uses her as a human guinea pig. Or maybe she's perfectly sane, but the Greedy Villain and the Corrupt Doctor conspire to drive her insane. Maybe she's perfectly sane when she arrives, but thinks she's going nuts because of the ghost's activities.

Examples from literature: In *Cousin Kate* by Georgette Heyer, young Torquil is mentally unstable and commits cruel atrocities during periods of insanity. In *Jane Eyre* by Charlotte Bronte, violently insane Bertha Mason is kept locked up in the attic by her husband, who hides her existence.

THE SEMI-OUTSIDER

This character is closely connected to the family but isn't part of it, and he knows the Gloomy House well but doesn't live there. He could be a distant cousin who grew up in the Gloomy House and still visits often. The MC doesn't know where the Semi-Outsider's loyalties lie. In Gothic Romance, he often turns out to be the Love Interest, and sometimes also the True Heir.

Example from Literature: In *Cousin Kate* by Georgette Heyer, Phillip Broome is a relative who knows the Gloomy House and everyone in it well, but he's doesn't live there and isn't part of the family.

THE ALLY OUTSIDE

The MC has a colleague, sister, friend, godmother or other friendly person who cares about her well-being but is not able to be with her in the Gloomy House. The Ally Outside may have initially encouraged the MC to take this job, or she may have warned her against it. Distance prevents the Ally Outside from providing real help, although she contrives at least one visit. The villain perceives this visit as a danger, so he makes sure the visit is a short one and the MC gets no chance to talk alone with the Ally Outside. In Romance novels, the Ally Outside can be the Love Interest. In this case, the Ally Outside contrives to visit in secret several times.

Examples from literature: In *Cousin Kate* by Georgette Heyer, Mrs Nidd used to be the MC's childhood nurse. She's the only one whom the MC can truly trust, but the villain intercepts their correspondence. In *The Gabriel Hounds* by Mary Stewart, the MC's cousin Charles knows that she has gone to the Gloomy House, but will he realise she is in danger, and will he gain access?

THE LOVE INTEREST

Many Gothic short stories (and almost all Gothic novels) contain a Romance element. The MC falls in love (possibly at first with the wrong person, then with the Love Interest who turns out to be her true love). Often, the Love Interest is the master of the Gloomy House, the Semi-Outsider, or the Ally Outside. The Love Interest could also be another newly-arrived outsider. They may arrive separately (she's a governess to the girls, he's the tutor to the boys) or together (they're newlyweds honeymooning in a remote castle).

Example from literature: Raoul de Valmy in *Nine Coaches Waiting* by Mary Stewart is a great example of a Love Interest character whose true nature is not revealed until the end. In many plot twists, the reader is led to believe him a noble hero and a ruthless villain in turns.

THE EVIL CHARMER

This character may make everyone – including the MC – like him and even fall in love with him. He then abuses their trust to his own ends. In some stories, he's not universally liked, but a ruthless seducer of members of the opposite sex, who – especially in Historical fiction – ruins women. Often, he's the master of the Gloomy House, but he could also be the visiting doctor or lawyer who seems on the MC's side. Maybe he appears likeable and charming in the first chapters before he shows his true colours, or perhaps people know that he's evil but still succumb to his demonic charm. The Evil Charmer could also be the Loyal Retainer, the Bigamist or the Semi-Outsider.

Example from literature: In Jane Austen's novel *Northanger Abbey*, dashing heir, Captain Frederick Tilney seduces an ambitious young woman by leading her to expect marriage.

THE GHOST

A ghost haunts the Gloomy House – probably the underground chamber, the attic, the staircase, a corridor or the picture gallery. She was either the victim or the perpetrator of a crime (most likely, murder, bigamy, deceit over the inheritance) and wants to get the old wrong righted. She may seek to redeem herself for her own misdeed, or she may seek vengeance on the descendants of the person who did her wrong. Sometimes, the evil deed committed by or against her is mirrored by the modern-day Guilty Secret.

Examples from literature: In *The Old Nurse's Story* by Elizabeth Gaskell, the ghost of a pretty little girl lures the child Rosamond out into the freezing cold. In *Nocturne for a Widow* by Amanda DeWees, the ghost of the late first wife slashes the dress the MC was going to wear to a special event – but does she mean to harm or to protect?

THE DOG

Surprisingly many works of Gothic Fiction feature a canine character. It can be a fierce guard dog or the master's faithful companion (in which case it takes on the role of Loyal Retainer). It might also be the Newly Arrived Outsider's beloved pet, or one of the Obsessed Scientist's laboratory animals. It might be a monster or the Ghost. The Dog likely has strong likes and dislikes, and it may notice suspicious smells or dig up a clue to the Guilty Secret.

Example from literature: The Dog in the Sherlock Holmes story *The Hound of the Baskervilles* by Arthur Conan Doyle is both a mythological beast and a real-life savage canine.

THE BLINKERED PROFESSIONAL

Thoroughly competent in his role, he unfortunately doesn't see the big picture. He carries out the task he's been hired for, and nothing else.

As a doctor, he refuses to prescribe the harmful medication to the Sickly Invalid or to sign the death certificate without an autopsy. As a lawyer, he refuses to issue illegal documents, and he even warns the bride that it's not in her interest to sign the prenuptial agreement. He remains firm, even under pressure from the villain – but with his duties concluded, he won't involve himself further.

When this person arrives on the scene, the MC is hopeful, believing that this unbiased expert will see the truth – but the Blinkered Professional isn't interested.

Example from literature: In *The Woman in White* by Wilkie Collins, lawyer Vincent Gilmore points out that the terms of the marriage contract are not in the bride's interest, and warns her guardian not to sign the agreement.

THE TRUE HEIR

He's the one who has inherited the Gloomy House, probably because of the Old Eccentric's bizarre will. He might also be the one who was defrauded of his inheritance (due to bigamy or some other crime). He may be the Helpless Child whose fate and fortune are in the hands of the Abusive Guardian. Or maybe he hasn't inherited yet, but stands to inherit, and his evil relatives want him out of the way before the wealthy Old Eccentric dies. In some novels, the Semi-Outsider, the Loyal Retainer, the Love Interest, the Newly Arrived Outsider and/or the MC herself turn out to be the True Heir.

Since the True Heir's identity is often revealed as a twist at the end of the book, I won't give examples from literature and spoil your reading surprise.

WHAT NOT TO DO

Don't populate your story with cardboard characters who represent a role but lack individual features. Use the archetypal energies of the character types I've introduced in this chapter, but flesh them out as real people. Don't leave them as mere stereotypes.

FURTHER STUDIES

If you want to delve further into this subject, my books *Writing Vivid Characters* and the more specialised *Writing About Villains*, both in the Writer's Craft series, will help you deepen your insights and broaden your skills.

ASSIGNMENTS

1. Think of a Gothic novel or story you've read (or a Gothic movie you've watched). Identify the 'types' you recognise from the list in this chapter. (You may be surprised how many you find.) Do any of the characters combine multiple 'types'?

2. Now look at your own story. Which types might suit your story? You don't need to include them all. Choose the ones that suit – and have fun combining several types in a single character. Feel free to come up with weird combinations. (What if the Corrupt Priest is the Bigamist, or the Dog is the True Heir? Bizarre combinations may spark original plot twists.)

CHAPTER 6

GUILTY SECRETS, SECRET GUILT

Secrets are at the core of Gothic Fiction. The plot often revolves around how the MC discovers a secret, and this discovery puts her in jeopardy. It is probably a terrible crime committed or planned by someone in the Gloomy House.

CRIMES AND CRIMINALS

The crime may have happened long ago, in the Old Eccentric's youth or even in a previous century, but it has repercussions on the modern characters. For example, if a last will and testament or a property deed were faked, the discovery of this secret may mean the current master of the Gloomy House does not really own the building.

The crime might also be currently ongoing, for example, the Gloomy House serves as the headquarters of a smuggling gang or as a holding centre for the trafficking of children into sexual slavery.

In some stories, the crime is planned for the future. The criminal plots to murder the True Heir or to commit bigamy with the Naive Bride.

Often, the crime is connected with an inheritance (e.g. a fake last will and testament) or bigamy. Murder (motivated by greed, passion or revenge) is always popular. Another possibility is drugs: trafficking, dealing, addiction, a corrupt doctor prescribing harmful drugs to a helpless patient. Smuggling, counterfeiting and burglary are also great options.

When writing Historical fiction (or referring to a crime committed in the past), it's worth researching the relevant laws of that time and that country. Don't assume that the inheritance and marital laws are the same everywhere in the world, or that laws have remained unchanged through centuries. Above all, don't assume that what you read in other novels must be true. You might inadvertently copy other writers' erroneous assumptions.

WHERE IS THE SECRET HIDDEN?

The secret itself (or clues to it) are almost certainly in the Gloomy House – most likely in the cellar or the attic. However, they could also be in the secret passage, in the library (a small piece of paper slipped between the pages of one of the ancient books) or in the ancestor's gallery (perhaps an old painting was overpainted with a different motif to hide the content). Sometimes, the secret is buried in a grave.

HOW IS THE SECRET REVEALED?

The main character stumbles upon a clue to the secret. She may overhear snatches of conversation or chat with gossiping neighbours, realise that something doesn't quite add up, and start to ask probing questions.

She may also discover something odd in the course of her work, for example, when renewing the plaster of the walls, restoring a painting in the ancestors' gallery, teaching the Helpless Child or caring for the Sickly Invalid. Her professional experience tells her that something is wrong, and she investigates.

At first, she doesn't realise what the oddity is about – but the discovery puts her in danger. To keep the secret, the criminals (or the criminals' descendants) will go to any length. They may try to kill her, or to drive her insane so her testimony won't be believed.

Another possibility is that the MC is an expert investigator – perhaps a private eye or ghost hunter – called in by another character who discovered a disturbing clue. When the MC arrives, she may find that this character has mysteriously vanished or died.

Piece by piece, the MC unravels the mystery, either on her own, or with the help of one or two other characters. Let her use the skills she acquired from her career, hobby, travel or life experience.

A SERVANT KNOWS

An employee (or slave, minion, poor relation, tenant or lower-class dependent) knows about the Guilty Secret. Out of love, loyalty or fear, he aids and abets the perpetrator, or he helps to keep the secret by hiding evidence and lying to the police.

This servant has probably been with the family for a long time. His own father may have served the current master's father.

The servant is loyal to the point of obsession… but to whom? The person who owns the servant's loyalty is not necessarily the criminal. Perhaps he's loyal to the master. But perhaps he disapproves of the current master's criminal activities, so he is loyal to the previous master's memory. Perhaps the servant is loyal to his late master's ghost. Or maybe he is loyal to the current master, who is the Sickly Invalid and must be spared the shock of discovering that his son is a vile criminal.

Because of this obsessive loyalty, the servant may go to great lengths to guard the Guilty Secret – although in some stories, his loyalty is the reason why he exposes the secret.

WHO ELSE KNOWS?

In a short story, you may not have many characters. But in a longer story or a novel, additional suspense arises from wondering who else is in on the secret. Whom can the main character trust?

WHAT'S THE OFFICIAL EXPLANATION?

The main character isn't the only one who notices something odd. The neighbours or staff also notice things, and quite regularly. Strange noises, perhaps, or the gas lamps suddenly dimming for no reason, or the window curtains of the supposedly empty attic moving.

How do the secret-keepers explain these things away? Maybe they spread rumours about a ghost haunting the attic of the west wing, or about rats in the basement. They may also say it's the wind, or that the old building is shifting on its foundations. Perhaps they've revived an old local legend about a vampire or a giant hound on the moors, and while they themselves claim not to believe in it, they make sure everyone else does.

MORE THAN ONE SECRET

You can enrich your story's texture by allowing several characters to harbour Guilty Secrets.

Perhaps a crime was committed in the past… and another is unfolding now. The two may be related, for example, the current master and his distant ancestor both engaged in some form of slave trade.

In a novel (especially a Cosy Mystery or a Thriller), several characters with Guilty Secrets provide red herrings which the MC must investigate.

SEXUAL DEPRAVITY

Sexual deviations play a big role in many Gothic novels. In the 19th century, when such topics were largely taboo, neither talked nor written about, the Gothic novel was startlingly frank. Authors included sexual deviations in part to shock and thrill their readers, and in part to draw attention to abuses which the public otherwise pretended did not exist.

If you wish, you can include sexual deviations in your story – either to titillate your readers (if you write Gothic Erotica) or to show the depravity of the villain, or to alert the reader to the sexual abuses and their effect on victims.

Consider what you want to achieve, and choose how to involve your MC – as a victim, witness or active participant. Also think carefully about how explicit and graphic to be in your descriptions. This depends on the taste of your target audience as well as and on the genre. For a Gothic Christian Inspirational Romance, it's probably best to merely mention what's going on, whereas the readers of Gothic Erotica want to experience the explicit action, and readers of Gothic Thriller desire graphic details.

When writing Historical Gothic Fiction, bear in mind that moral standards have changed. You need to consider both modern sensibilities and the attitudes of the period. For example, the sexual abuse of children, which arouses outrage in modern readers, was tolerated in some periods of history, if the children were the abuser's slaves or belonged to the servant class.

On the other hand, homosexuality is no longer the shocking crime it once was. In many sectors of society, a man can simply come out as gay, and his nature will be fully accepted or at least grudgingly tolerated. But in the past, when homosexuality was punishable by prison or death, a gay man might go to desperate lengths to keep his secret.

PROFESSIONAL TIP

For emotional depth, give the MC a Guilty Secret, too. Her heavy conscience and fear of exposure make it impossible for her to investigate and expose someone else's crime. At the end of your story, your MC may gain redemption through a heroic deed.

While the MC investigating and surviving someone else's crime makes an entertaining but probably shallow yarn; if she has to deal with her own guilt, this creates a faceted, meaningful, memorable story.

WHAT NOT TO DO

Don't write a story in which the secret is easily uncovered. Instead, give several characters a vested interest in preserving the secret.

ASSIGNMENTS

1. What is the Guilty Secret? If you're not sure yet, think about what kind of discovery the main character may make in the cause of her work.

2. Whose secret is it? What would happen to them if the secret were found out? (For example, if it were discovered that their father committed bigamy, they may not be his legal heirs, and stand to lose their fortune.)

3. Who is in on the secret? Maybe the housekeeper knows, or the doctor is paid to keep quiet.

4. What's the first clue the main character finds? Where and how does she find it? What does she think it means? Whom does she tell about it?

5. Does the MC herself have a guilty secret to hide? What is it? What would happen if she were found out?

CHAPTER 7

DRIVING PASSIONS AND OBSESSIONS

Gothic Fiction is intense. Emotions run high, and characters go to any length to satisfy their passions and obsessions.

Passion is a strong, barely controllable emotion about an issue, person or pursuit. Often, passion is connected with relationship matters, and it's an amplified version of a 'normal' feeling such as love, hatred, jealousy, desire. Passion intensifies that emotion so much that the person has difficulty making rational, ethical choices. Sometimes, suppressed passions (such as the forbidden love for a married woman or the sexual desire for a sibling) smoulder and increase, and then suddenly explode. In the grip of passion, people do things they later regret, such as have unprotected sex, marry the wrong man or commit a crime.

Obsession is a mental state where thoughts about an issue, person or pursuit fill the mind constantly to a troubling extent. In the grip of obsession, a person loses judgment of what is important and what isn't, and may make choices that a rational person would disdain – such as sell his daughter to obtain the rare ruby he wants for his gemstone collection, or infect humans with incurable diseases so he can use them as guinea pigs in his quest for a cure.

Passion and obsession overlap. They may occur simultaneously, and one may lead to the other.

CHARACTERS AND THEIR PASSIONS

In Gothic Fiction, every character can have a passion or obsession. The villain certainly has one – and it is what drives him to commit the evil deeds. He may have had ethical scruples initially, but he has long set them aside. He'll do what it takes to get the woman he desires, to complete his collection of rare artefacts, to wreak vengeance on the people who wronged him long ago. The villain's passion or obsession is probably closely interwoven with the Guilty Secret.

The MC probably has a passion, too. Her passion should be for an honourable cause of which the reader can approve. She will try to stay ethical and maintain her integrity, but she may be seriously tempted to transgress. In some stories, she gives in to the temptation and commits a crime or grievous sin which later weighs on her conscience, and the plot revolves around her quest for redemption and her need to right the wrongs.

The easiest technique is to make the MC emotionally passionate about an aspect of her work. If she's a dancer, make her passionate about music or dance. If she's a governess, make her passionate about childcare or education.

Every character in your story can have a passion or obsession, as long as it contributes to the plot. This adds entertainment, tension and intensity.

Let's say the housekeeper in the Gloomy House is a minor character. What if she's obsessed about guarding the silverware and keeps counting the knives every morning and night? What if one is missing before breakfast that definitely was in its drawer the night before?

Or what if she's passionate about keeping the floors spotless, and suddenly she discovers a faint trace of mud outside the laboratory, at a time when nobody was supposed to be in that part of the house?

Her passion may revolve around the butler. Deep down she knows that he's a bad man whom she should not trust... but when he flatters and seduces her, she forgets her promise to guard the child.

Obsession can be a symptom of mental problems, such as chronic anxiety or obsessive-compulsive disorder. Insanity is one of the tropes of Gothic Fiction. Perhaps a character's obsession at first seems a harmless eccentricity, but then spirals out of control, and others realise too late that he is criminally insane.

PROFESSIONAL TIP

Where appropriate, escalate feelings to passions, and interests to obsessions. Infuse every scene with some kind of passion.

WHAT NOT TO DO

Don't let anyone have lukewarm feelings or half-hearted interests – at any rate, not for long.

FURTHER STUDY

My book *Writing Vivid Emotions* can help you convey characters' passions.

ASSIGNMENTS

1. Give the villain of the story a passion or obsession. Think about the lengths to which he will go to satisfy it. In what way does this feed into the Guilty Secret?

2. Give the MC a passion – probably one the reader can approve of. In what way does this passion drive her into action and investigation? How does it keep her going when someone else would have given up?

3. Now look at the rest of the characters, and brainstorm ideas for their passions and obsessions. Ideally, each character should have at least one passion or obsession, but you don't need to decide them all yet. At this stage, simply gather ideas. You can decide later, when fleshing out the story.

CHAPTER 8

HOW TO START AND END YOUR STORY

By now you should have at least a vague idea for your story's plot. Perhaps the plot is quite clear in your mind already and just needs fine-tuning as it unfolds. But perhaps the events and structure are still hazy. Either is fine.

I'm going to show you the points where Gothic stories typically start and end. These openings and endings may suit your story. If yes, use them, and you may find that once those two points are fixed, the rest of the plot falls into place.

However, if a different beginning or ending suits your story better, run with it. Not every Gothic story has to start and finish at these points.

HOW TO BEGIN THE SHORT STORY

The main character (MC) arrives at the Gloomy House. She sees it for the first time, feels overwhelmed, grateful and daunted. She perceives it has her salvation, but also senses a menace.

Her employer/her host/a servant receives her. She sees part of the interior and takes up residence.

HOW TO BEGIN THE NOVEL

The novel starts earlier. In the first scene, show the MC in dire straits, trying to get out of a hole. Perhaps she's run out of money and desperately tries to find a job. Her attempts are unsuccessful. She has run out of options when the unexpected invitation/job offer/assignment to the Gloomy House arrives. It's her only chance, so she suppresses her misgivings and accepts. The second scene features her arrival at Gloomy House.

HOW TO END THE SHORT STORY

The building gets destroyed in a dramatic way. It may burn to the ground, collapse in an earthquake, get washed away in a tsunami. The house's evil content (the torture chamber, the cursed painting) vanishes forever.

The MC may be inside (perhaps locked in the cellar or the attic) and barely escapes with her life. Alternatively, she may be outside and safe, but heroically dashes into the danger to save someone's life. She may also watch the building's destruction from a distance.

Often, the villain perishes in the disaster – perhaps because he tried to salvage the infernal machine or his ill-gotten wealth – or because he deliberately risks his life to save someone else's, thus partially redeeming himself in death.

Sometimes, a good character also dies, and this adds a sad note to what might otherwise be an over-sweet ending.

HOW TO END THE NOVEL

The building's dramatic destruction happens in the same way as described for the short story ending, but at the novel's climax rather than in the final scene. This is followed by one or more scenes during which things get wrapped up – for example, the police arrest the evildoers, and the lovers declare their love for each other and get engaged.

Often, there is an epilogue, showing the main character years later, when she is either happy in her new life, or filled with regrets. The site where the Gloomy House once stood may also feature in the epilogue. It appears that nobody alive, other than the MC, knows or remembers what really happened in that house.

PROFESSIONAL TIP

End the book on an intense emotional note.

WHAT NOT TO DO

Avoid slow, dragging beginnings with a lot of explanations, flashbacks and infodumps. Instead, get the MC to the Gloomy House as soon as possible, throw her into the situation, and rouse the reader's emotions from the first page.

ASSIGNMENTS

1. Summarise in a few sentences what happens in the first scene of your story. If you're writing a short story, consider making this the MC's arrival at the Gloomy House. You don't have to commit to this beginning and may amend it later if you wish.

2. Summarise in a few sentences what happens in your story's final scene. For a short story, this is probably the destruction of the Gloomy House, although you can choose a different ending.

CHAPTER 9

PLOT YOUR GOTHIC NOVEL WITH THE HERO'S JOURNEY

'The Hero's Journey' is a plot structure that underlies many of the most successful myths and novels of all times – from Homer's Odyssey to the latest bestsellers. Joseph Campbell (1904-1987) identified the elements and plot structure, and he gave 'The Hero's Journey' its name. Novelists and screenwriters have applied it ever since and found it a powerful tool for structuring their stories.

For Gothic novels, the Hero's Journey works particularly well. Experiment with using it as a scaffold for building your own novel.

Here are the typical sections, and my suggestions on how to interpret them in a Gothic novel.

1. THE ORDINARY WORLD

The MC is in her accustomed world. The reader gets to know her situation (perhaps penniless, in desperate need of a job or a home), her personality (plucky, honest, unafraid of hard work), her skills and her values. You may want to devote a chapter to this, showing her struggles to save money and her endeavours to get a job or assignment.

2. THE CALL TO ADVENTURE

A 'herald' arrives telling the 'hero' that he must go on a quest. In the Gothic novel, this is often a letter informing the MC that she has inherited a property in the middle of nowhere, the offer of a job (perhaps as a governess) or a major freelance assignment that requires her to stay on the site. She has mixed feelings. On the one hand, it's exciting and exactly what she needs. On the other hand, the prospect worries her, perhaps because of the remote location, because the house or the people have a sinister reputation, or perhaps simply because it sounds too good to be true.

3. REFUSAL OF THE CALL

At first, the MC doesn't want to go and flat out refuses. Why? Perhaps she doesn't want to accept charity. Maybe she hates the thought of being a poor relation in a wealthy family. She may not have the right qualifications and experience this job seems to require. Or perhaps she is retired and doesn't want to work in that field again.

But she soon learns that she must go. Perhaps the people with whom she's been staying aren't able to accommodate her any longer. Maybe someone (the Helpless Child or the Sickly Invalid) needs her help, and she feels obliged to provide it because of a promise made long ago or in return for a kindness once rendered to her parents. Or maybe something about the project sparks her curiosity. So she says yes.

4. MEETING THE MENTOR

In this section, the MC gets valuable advice from a knowledgeable, wise person. She may consult a freelancer in the same field who knows something about the Gloomy House, or she may get tips on how to educate a mentally unstable child, or whatever her job requires.

The mentor (the experienced colleague, subject expert or native of that country) tries to dissuade her from going, warning her of the dangers.

In most Gothic novels, this section is short, and you can skip it altogether.

5. PREPARING FOR THE JOURNEY

The MC gets ready for the adventure:

She researches the location, architecture and history of the Gloomy House, and is frustrated by how little she can discover. She may spend her last money on buying the kind of clothes she'll need. Perhaps she gets some magical, paranormal or spiritual item or blessing (perhaps something that had belonged to her family, and that will later identify her as the True Heir). She may obtain a special 'weapon' (in the Gothic Fiction context, this may be a tool used in her trade). She will also say farewell to a loved one – perhaps her only surviving sister, or the only friend she has left in this cruel world.

Depending on your plot, this section may take up several scenes, or you can condense it into a single paragraph.

6. CROSSING THE THRESHOLD

In the Hero's Journey, this is when the MC enters a new kind of world – another country, a new type of business. In the Gothic Novel, this is when she arrives at the Gloomy House.

There is often a 'gatekeeper' who tries to stop her, or at least slows her progress and delays her entry. In the Gothic novel, this could be a ferocious dog attacking her at the entrance (and later plays a role in the plot as the Dog), or it could be a receptionist who demands to see proof that she really has a booking, or a servant (maybe the Loyal Retainer) who is clearly reluctant to let her in.

This section plays a huge role in the Gothic novel, so make the most of it. I suggest that you devote a full chapter to it. For ideas how to develop it, see the chapter 'Arrival at the Gloomy House'.

7. LEARNING THE RULES OF THE NEW WORLD

Now the MC is in the new world, and she has to learn how everything works here. This is another important section in the Gothic novel, so make the most of it. It may spread over several scenes.

The MC may have to make sense of the customs and rituals, get acquainted with the weird people who live there, grasp hidden meanings of what is said, learn who is who and who has power, make sense of the hidden hierarchy among the servants, discover what's taboo and must never be talked about.

Show her struggling, making mistakes, unwittingly causing offence, getting robbed or ripped off, learning and adapting. All along, she picks up clues that something is wrong... but she's so confused, she can't assess whether it's true evil or whether she is imagining things.

8. THE TRAIL OF TRIALS

In Gothic Fiction, this section is often interwoven with the previous one. The MC gets tested somehow – perhaps there's a stern interview with her new employer, or maybe an emergency requires her to apply her skills.

In the Hero's Journey, the MC makes an enemy and gains allies in this section. This applies in Gothic Fiction... except that the MC can't be sure who the enemy is and who is an ally. More about this in the chapter 'Trust No One: Suspicion, Resentment and Betrayal'.

The MC often gets a new outfit or costume. This could be a beautiful new gown to wear at the upcoming ball... but it could also be an old dress that used to belong to an ancestress or a uniform worn by her predecessor in the job.

9. APPROACH TO THE INNERMOST CAVE

The MC enters a danger zone – the Obsessed Scientist's laboratory, the religious cult's secret initiation chamber.

The 'innermost cave' in the Hero's Journey is often set underground. This makes it a perfect match for the Gothic novel, because the Gloomy House usually has some kind of underground chamber.

This is a section of slow pace and high suspense. Stretch it out, and keep the reader on the edge of her seat. If your plot allows, devote several paragraphs or even a whole scene to this. What might happen on the way there? Perhaps she has to pacify the hostile dog, or hide in an alcove while the Loyal Retainer walks past. If it suits your story, use sensory impressions to create a creepy atmosphere.

10. THE ORDEAL

Now we've reached around the midpoint of the novel. The MC suffers physical, mental or emotional pain – or all three. Perhaps she believes that she's going insane, or witnesses her lover getting engaged to another woman, or maybe the villain is torturing her to make her sign a false statement.

Make this experience as painful and scary as your story and genre allow.

If you want to give your novel a 'Black Moment' (a scene when all seems lost), place it in this section.

You can give the scene poignancy by making the suffering voluntary. For example, the MC may suffer torture rather than reveal the secret, or she may allow herself to be abused in order to buy time for the Helpless Child to escape.

Sometimes the Approach to the Innermost Cave and the Ordeal are not physical actions but a descent into the dark part of the MC's own psyche. In Gothic Fiction, this facet works especially well.

Perhaps the MC's Guilty Secret, conflicting loyalties, suppressed desires or barely controlled lust for vengeance bring out her dark side.

11. THE INITIATION

This can be a positive or a negative event – but it is definitely an intense experience which transforms the MC somehow.

In Gothic Fiction, this initiation is often related to the paranormal, the supernatural, or death. Perhaps there's a ritual to call upon the spirit of ancestors or to raise a corpse, or maybe a séance to communicate with the dead, or a ceremony to gain a glimpse of the future. Maybe the MC gets initiated into a secret society or cult. The ritual may have sexual undertones.

As part of the initiation, the MC may have to bring a major sacrifice or surrender herself in some way, and she may be granted something precious. Does she undergo this ritual willingly, or has she been forced or manipulated into it?

She may experience a form of death and rebirth, either symbolically or physically or both. Physically, this often means a near-fatal injury or a near-fatal event, perhaps the direct consequence of the ordeal, or an accident during her attempted escape.

If your story allows, make your MC lose consciousness for a while. Perhaps she faints because the horrible thing she sees is more than she can bear, or the time travel knocked her out, or she lost so much blood during the ordeal that she passed out. She might also survive a murder attempt that leaves her comatose for days.

Whatever happens, when she regains her consciousness, physically and/or symbolically, she is changed – probably wiser, but perhaps insane. The transformation is crucial.

12. SEIZING THE PRIZE

The MC now takes something precious and carries it away with her. In ancient myths, this is often a magic elixir or a special sword. In Gothic Fiction, it may be evidence of the Guilty Secret or the crimes committed in the Gloomy House. It may also be the missing Last Will and Testament, a secret letter, or a work of art.

The MC probably found this special something in the innermost cave during the Ordeal or Initiation.

13. THE ROAD BACK

In the Hero's Journey, the MC takes that seized prize back to the 'ordinary world' where it is needed or where it belongs. In Gothic novels, the MC may escape from the Gloomy House, endeavouring to bring the evidence to the authorities.

But the journey back is not smooth. The evil villain won't simply put up with the loss, but goes after the MC to get it back – and in Gothic Fiction, he usually succeeds. The MC often doesn't make it far. She just believes herself safe when she gets recaptured and returned to captivity in the Gloomy House.

In this section, there's often a betrayal. Someone the MC thought of as an ally turns against her and sides with the villain, and that's how the MC gets recaptured just when she thought herself safe.

14. RESURRECTION

This section is the Climax (or a Climax) of the story. In some ways, it is similar to the 'Approach to the Innermost Cave—Ordeal—Initiation' sequence, but things happen much faster. You may have high speed action here.

There's often a confrontation with the villain, complete with physical fighting. If the MC has already defeated the villain earlier, then the villain comes back, set on getting revenge as well as on retrieving the prize.

The MC may also realise that the baddie she defeated was just a lieutenant, and now finds out who the real evil mastermind is – probably someone she liked and trusted.

This is a good scene in which to place the destruction of the Gloomy House – see the chapter 'Dramatic Demise: The Destruction of the Gloomy House' for suggestions.

Perhaps the MC is trapped inside the burning or collapsing house and nearly dies. This is the MC's second almost-death in the novel, and often a metaphorical or ritual purification takes place as the hero is 'resurrected'.

The Climax in Gothic novels is rich in both action and emotion.

15. ARRIVAL BACK HOME

As the MC re-enters the Ordinary World, she has to remember or even re-learn the once-familiar rules of the Ordinary World which now may strike her as petty or strange. She may settle comfortably into her old routines, or she may chafe at the restrictions and yearn for the freedom and adventure of her quest. She has certainly grown wiser. She reunites with the 'loved one' – her sister or only friend.

However, in Gothic Fiction, this section is short – and it's not necessarily the end. The MC may have found her true vocation or true love, and goes where her job or new husband take her. In some books she becomes the new mistress of the Gloomy House, assuming that it hasn't been destroyed.

CREATIVE FREEDOM

Use the Hero's Journey as a scaffold to support your story, not as a cage to confine it.

In your novel, you may have all these parts or only some of them, and they don't necessarily happen in exactly this order. Even the ancient myths don't all use the structure as it is. It's quite flexible, so adapt it. Sometimes several of these stages happen simultaneously, or one may be much longer than all the others.

PROFESSIONAL TIP

If you've already written a draft of a novel, you can use the structure of the Hero's Journey to refine it. Instead of structuring your whole book with this model, pick a section which needs more drama and depth. Consider which of the stages of the Hero's Journey it might correspond to, and use this for inspiration.

WHAT NOT TO DO

Don't stick slavishly to the structure of the Hero's Journey plot model, because that can lead to hackneyed plots, especially in Epic Fantasy fiction. Instead, bend and shape it to suit your vision.

FURTHER STUDY

My book *Writing Vivid Plots* looks in more depth at the Hero's Journey and other plot models, as well as many advanced techniques for fiction plotting.

If you're particularly interested in the Hero's Journey, I suggest you read Joseph Campbell's 1949 work, *The Hero with a Thousand Faces*. I also recommend *The Writer's Journey: Mythic Structure for Writers* by Christopher Vogler (an in-depth work), and *The Key: How to Write Damn Good Fiction Using the Power of Myth* by James N. Frey (a to-the-point guide). For those interested in gender studies, you can find online articles and books exploring the (possibly different) journeys of female heroes.

ASSIGNMENT

If you're writing or revising a novel, gather ideas of what happens at each stage of the Hero's Journey.

CHAPTER 10

STRUCTURING YOUR SHORT STORY WITH PLOT EVENTS

The Hero's Journey plot model rarely works for short stories. It's simply too long. Fewer things happen in a short story, and the events unfold over a much shorter period.

I find it useful to work with 'Plot Events'. These are the things that happen in the story.

By now, you probably have a good idea of what happens in your story, even if you don't have a clear plot yet. So let's go through it step-by-step.

1. Start by making a list of everything you want to happen – just a few words for instance, no details.

2. Sort these events in approximate chronological order.

3. Place what you've decided to be the 'beginning' and the 'ending' of your story first and last.

4. Now turn each item in the list into a sentence describing a 'Plot Event'. Later in this chapter, I'll show you how to do this. It's possible that some items on your list of incidents will break down into several Plot Events each, while others will combine several items into just one Plot Event.

5. Now read what you've written – it's basically a draft synopsis of your story. It probably still has some weaknesses – perhaps there are plot holes, maybe the middle sags, a major issue isn't clear yet, or the ending doesn't have enough action.

6. Brainstorm ideas for fixing those problems.

7. Now rewrite your synopsis, keeping it as a list of Plot Events.

8. Decide on the time frame. Does the story unfold over a week or in a single afternoon? Tip: The tighter the time frame, the better. In a novel, you can spread events out over weeks, months or even years, but short stories work best if they cover only a short period.

9. Decide whether to tell the story in chronological order, or whether the story will jump forward or back in time. Tip: For most stories, the chronological order works best. Stick to it unless you're certain that a different approach will serve the story better.

10. Group the Plot Events into scenes. Whenever there's a natural break (perhaps because the location changes or time passes) insert a scene break.

11. Now you have a structured point-by-point synopsis. This is called the 'outline'. When you're mostly happy with the outline (it doesn't need to be perfect yet), you're ready to write the first draft of your story.

HOW TO DEVELOP PLOT EVENTS

A Plot Event is an incident happening in a story.

Here are examples of Plot Events:

*   Mary resists the Evil Charmer's attempts at seduction.

*   When the Old Eccentric dies, the potential heirs try to (or pretend to try to) find the will.

*   While restoring an old book, Mary finds a Last Will and Testament between its pages.

*   Fleeing from the attic, Mary knocks over a candle and sets the building aflame.

It's important that every Plot Event needs to be an 'event' – i.e. something must happen.

The MC thinking, wondering, realising, remembering, considering, or feeling is **not** a Plot Event. However, realisations and emotions can be incorporated into Plot Events as triggers or consequences.

Examples:

Mary realises that the Corrupt Doctor tries to poison her aunt is not a Plot Event.

When Mary realises that the Corrupt Doctor tries to poison her aunt, she switches the medicine bottles is a Plot Event.

Mary feels angry is not a Plot Event.

*Mary discovers John's deception and feels angry i*s a Plot Event.

John believes that Mary is in love with the Semi-Outsider is not a Plot Event.

Believing that Mary is in love with the Semi-Outsider, John breaks off their engagement is a Plot Event.

Include only the most important developments as Plot Events, and leave out details, descriptions, backstory and explanations. Keep it simple!

Stories can have any number of Plot Events. Some have only five, others may have fifty-five. The more plot events, the longer the story.

PROFESSIONAL TIP

Use as few characters as possible in your short story, because too large a cast could cause confusion especially where characters have a similar role in the story or have little to distinguish between them.

Gothic Fiction makes it easy to reduce the cast by combining roles, so if you have too many characters, simply combine them. The Corrupt Doctor is also the Obsessed Scientist and the Ghost, while the Semi-Outsider is also the Blinkered Professional and the True Heir.

WHAT NOT TO DO

Don't include details (character profiles, setting descriptions etc.) in your outline.

FURTHER STUDY

You may find my book *Writing Vivid Plots* useful.

ASSIGNMENT

1. Write a list of Plot Events for your story, arrange them in the order you want them to unfold, and group them into scenes. Remember to keep the Plot Events simple (free from background information and details), and make sure that something happens in each Plot Event.

2. Revise the resulting outline until you feel that it conveys a story you want to tell.

CHAPTER 11

STIRRING UP INNER AND OUTER CONFLICTS

Your story needs at least one outer and one inner conflict for the MC. The outer conflict makes the story exciting; the inner conflict makes it meaningful.

Most works of Gothic Fiction – especially novels – have more conflicts, but let's look at these two first.

THE OUTER CONFLICT

The central outer conflict is what drives the action. It's between the MC and another person (the antagonist), or between two groups of people, one of which includes the MC. Sometimes the MC and the antagonist have goals which are incompatible (only one of the two can succeed). Perhaps she wants to protect the dune that's home to an endangered species, while he wants to destroy it to build a hotel on the land. In other novels, the MC and the antagonist both want the same thing, but only one can win. For example, both want to inherit the Gloomy House, or both want to marry the same man.

The outer conflict typically gets resolved with action in the Climax.

A facet unique to Gothic Fiction is that the MC often doesn't know with whom she is in conflict. She realises that someone opposes her, but for a long time doesn't know who is on her side and who is the enemy.

THE INNER CONFLICT

This is what gives the novel depth and emotional impact. It's a fight inside the MC, between two things she holds dear – values, loyalties, beliefs. She tries to hold on to both, but they tear her apart.

Here are some examples:

- Loyalty to her late grandmother versus loyalty to her employer

- Religious faith versus love for a man

- Integrity versus ambition

- Love versus loyalty

- Love versus sanctity of marriage

She may have to make a tough choice between the two, sacrificing one value in order to protect the other. In Gothic novels, she may initially just compromise one of them, soothing her conscience by convincing herself that it's just a small thing. But instead of abating, the conflict intensifies. It's typical of Gothic novel plots that the MC has to make several painful decisions. The most heart-wrenching of these often comes immediately before the novel's climax.

The inner conflict is often the theme of the story.

EXAMPLE

Let's say you're writing a Gothic Thriller. The MC is Mary, a retired senior police officer, widowed, holidaying in a vacation camp on a remote island. She realises the camp serves as a cover for child trafficking.

The outer conflict is between Mary, who wants to end the child trafficking, and the criminal mastermind. For a long time, Mary doesn't know who he (or she) is.

Her inner conflict may be that she doesn't want to get involved with investigations again, perhaps because of a promise she has made to her late husband, or because she is ill and the doctors have warned her that the excitement of another investigation will seriously harm her health.

ADDITIONAL CONFLICTS

You can add further layers of inner and outer conflicts, some of which may last for several chapters, others only for one scene. Relate them to the main conflicts.

Let's take the example of the vacationing ex-police officer Mary.

Maybe the hotel management puts her into a cramped room with a single window looking out onto a concrete wall although she paid for a luxury suite with a sea view and balcony. This puts her in conflict with the management.

Perhaps she falls in love – and she realises this is the true love she's been waiting for all her life. But the man is married, and Mary believes in the sanctity of marriage. Now there is an additional conflict between her value and her love.

In a short story, just one outer and one inner conflict may be sufficient, but in a novel, you can pile the conflicts on.

OTHER CHARACTERS' CONFLICTS

Ideally, every character in the novel should be in conflict with someone, something or themselves. Conflicts about loyalty, compassion and ambition abound. Faced with tough choices, the characters will not always make the decision the MC expects them to.

Let the other characters' conflicts represent a facet of the MC's own. If she struggles between loyalty and compassion, the other characters may have conflicts relating to loyalty or compassion, too. This gives your novel depth.

PROFESSIONAL TIP

Create suspense by not revealing immediately who the MC's opponent in the main outer conflict is. Build additional tension by revealing only gradually what the other characters' conflicts are.

WHAT NOT TO DO

Don't write a story containing only inner conflict – this would be boring to read.

Don't write a story containing only outer conflict. Although this could still be exciting to read, it would feel shallow and forgettable.

FURTHER STUDIES

My book *Writing Vivid Plots* explores ways to use different types of conflicts in fiction.

ASSIGNMENTS

1. Give your MC several conflicts – at least one outer and one inner conflict.

2. Look at your list of characters, and try to give each at least one conflict. Minor characters may have just an outer conflict, but your story will gain depth if several characters have inner conflicts as well.

CHAPTER 12

REAL AND UNREAL, GOOD AND EVIL

Gothic Fiction deals with opposites: good and evil, real and unreal, past and present, truth and lies, sanity and insanity, tradition and modernity, justice and injustice....

Often, it explores the edges where the two extremes meet. Sometimes, there is a clear boundary (perhaps symbolised by a portal), at other times, there's an area where the two opposites blend into each other (like day bleeding into night, or night diffusing into day, which is why twilight is frequently used as a metaphor).

GOOD AND EVIL IN CHARACTERS

In the earliest Gothic Fiction, e.g. *The Castle of Otranto* by Horace Walpole, good and evil are clearly defined. People are good or bad, and act accordingly. But many novels use more complex characterisation. There is good in evil people, and evil in good. Both natures are genuine.

For example, the man who is unscrupulous about destroying an endangered species to enrich himself works tirelessly to rescue abused children.

This dual nature makes it difficult for the MC to know whom to like and trust, and can mislead her about someone's intentions. She may love the old lady who runs an animal rescue shelter, and support her work... not realising until the end that this is the criminal mastermind behind the child trafficking.

REALITY VERSUS IMAGINATION

When strange incidents happen, the MC struggles to make sense of them. There may be only two explanations: either supernatural forces are at work, or she is imagining things. Either is possible in Gothic Fiction. Ghosts, vampires, demons and other creatures can populate your novel.

But it can be the MC's imagination. Perhaps the MC is overwrought and prone to seeing things that aren't there – after all, she's recently been diagnosed with a mental disorder, and gone to the Gloomy House to recuperate, so perhaps some strange perceptions are to be expected.

Perhaps the MC's own guilty conscience creates the visions – think of Edgar Allan Poe's *The Tell-Tale Heart*.

Or perhaps she's a creative type with a vivid imagination. Catherine Morland in Jane Austen's *Northanger Abbey* is a teenager with decidedly Gothic fantasies, and she suspects sinister goings on in everything.

Other characters in the story may deliberately fire up the imagination. They may even plant rumours about a ghost or mythological monster to create a smokescreen for their criminal activities and keep people from investigating. Example from literature: the monstrous hound from Sir Arthur Conan Doyle's *The Hound of the Baskervilles*.

Worse, the villain may deliberately create bizarre experiences and mislead the MC until she doubts her own perception – and he may even drive her insane. Example from literature: Patrick Hamilton's play *Gas Light*, and its subsequent film adaptations under the title *Gaslight*.

AMBIGUITY

In some masterpieces of Gothic Fiction, the reader is left wondering what was real and what was the MC's imagination.

Here are famous examples from literature:

The Turn of the Screw by Henry James. Academics have analysed this story over and over, trying to decide whether the children were really possessed or whether it all was in the governess' imagination. More than 200 years after publication, the debate is as intense as ever.

My Cousin Rachel by Daphne du Maurier. The question hinges on the character of Rachel: is she a grieving widow or a scheming murderess? The MC, Philip, is convinced sometimes of one, then of the other, and wavers between the two. In the end, he causes her death. Has he executed his uncle's vile killer, or has he murdered an innocent? The author deliberately provided clues for both, so there will never be a definite answer, and the question will forever remain in the minds of people who read the book.

The Haunting of Hill House by Shirley Jackson. Taking part in a psychic research project, MC Eleanor gradually becomes possessed by the house – or is she simply an emotionally disturbed woman? Are the events real, do they exist only in Eleanor's imagination, or are they actually caused by her telekinetic ability? The story allows different interpretations.

The kind of ambiguity that leaves the reader wondering about the question yet satisfied within the book requires great literary skill. It's definitely not a project for novices, but if you're a skilled writer, this can be a novel with which to make your mark.

PROFESSIONAL TIP

A relatively easy – but highly effective – way to handle the good-versus-evil concept is to give each of the bad characters a genuinely good facet. This serves to misdirect the MC and the readers, and it adds depth to the story.

WHAT NOT TO DO

Don't make it absolutely clear who is good or bad, and what is real or unreal – at least not immediately. Keep the MC and the readers guessing for a while.

FURTHER STUDIES

My books *Writing Vivid Characters* and *Writing About Villains* both guide you deeper into this subject.

ASSIGNMENT

Create a situation in your story where something is not what it seems to be. Perhaps the supposed 'haunting' is really the activity of a living criminal, or maybe the opposite is true: the supposed crimes are really the doings of a ghost. Or maybe a supposedly good person is really evil, or a supposedly evil villain is really a good guy. Choose any one of the elements discussed in this chapter, and find a way to incorporate it into your plot.

Who has an interest in keeping up the smokescreen? When does the MC first get an inkling of the truth? When and how does she find out the whole truth?

CHAPTER 13

GETTING DEEP INTO THE EXPERIENCE: POINT OF VIEW

From whose perspective are you telling the story? Will the reader slip inside the head of the MC and see everything through her eyes only? Or will you switch perspectives, inviting the reader to experience events through a different person in each chapter? Maybe you prefer a different approach altogether.

The great thing about Gothic Fiction is that it offers complete flexibility about Point-of-View (PoV). You can choose whichever perspective (or perspectives) you feel most comfortable with, and use what suits your story best.

Here are the three main choices:

SINGLE LIMITED POV

The reader is inside the MC's head for the duration of the story, experiencing what she does, seeing through her eyes, hearing through her ears, suffering her pains, feeling her emotions, thinking her thoughts.

This approach has enormous pulling-in power. It encourages the reader to 'become' the character while reading and become totally immersed in the experience. You can even take it further and use deep PoV, which is single limited PoV so intense that the reader forgets that it's a story and feels like it's happening to her.

The drawback is that you can only show what the MC experiences. You can't take the reader to another town to show how her sister is getting on, or expose the Obsessed Scientist torturing animals in his laboratory unless the MC is there to watch it.

The point of view character is almost always the MC. The story can be told in first person ('I arrived at sunset.') or third person ('She arrived at sunset.')

If you want to study this form of PoV in depth, you may find my book *Writing Deep Point of View: Professional Techniques for Fiction Authors* helpful.

Example from literature: *Jane Eyre* by Charlotte Bronte. Jane is the MC and PoV character, and the story is narrated by her in first person. The reader experiences only what Jane does.

SERIAL LIMITED POV (ALSO CALLED 'MULTIPLE POV')

In this approach, you let the reader experience the story from several different characters' perspective, one at a time.

You can tell each chapter from someone else's PoV, or alternate between the MC and the villain.

This gives you a wider storytelling scope than the single limited PoV, but the emotional experience for the reader isn't quite as intense.

Wait for a natural break in the story (for example, the end of a chapter or a scene) before switching to the next PoV. Avoid switching PoV in the middle of a scene.

Example from literature: *The Woman in White* by Wilkie Collins. This story switches between the narratives of several characters. The first chapter begins in the PoV of the MC, art teacher Walter Hartright. Later chapters switch to perspective of other characters, such as Marian Halcombe, Frederick Fairlie, and others. The ending is again in the MC's PoV.

OMNISCIENT POV

With this god-like perspective, the reader can look into everyone's heart and soul at once. With your guidance, the reader can experience what goes on in the MC's mind and the villain's at the same time.

Omniscient PoV follows one character for a few paragraphs, then another, and in between it makes statements about the whole world. It may even deliver historical information, spell out the author's moral comments or look into the future.

This allows a broad scope for storytelling, but prevents emotional immersion. The reader stays detached, aware that this is merely a story.

Omniscient PoV was popular in the 18th and 19th century, so many of the early Gothic novels use it. Today's readers tend to prefer the emotional intensity of single or serial PoV. However, omniscient PoV still works well for Gothic Fiction.

Example from literature: *Northanger Abbey* by Jane Austen is in omniscient PoV. The MC is Catherine Morland. The reader watches Catherine's adventures sometimes from inside her head, sometimes from an outsider's perspective. There are also authorial comments and sweeping statements that work only in omniscient PoV, such as 'It would be mortifying to the feelings of many ladies, could they be made to understand how little the heart of a man is affected by what is costly or new in their attire.'

PROFESSIONAL TIPS

For single limited PoV, it's worth going all the way and making it deep PoV, to create a total immersion and an intense experience for the reader.

When writing serial limited PoV, avoid the reader's feeling disoriented. At the beginning of each scene, immediately establish for the reader whose head she is in.

To make omniscient PoV work, stay in each character's perspective for a short time, avoid changing the PoV in mid-paragraph, and insert at least one PoV-neutral sentence before you enter the next character's head.

WHAT NOT TO DO

Avoid head-hopping (jumping from one perspective to another) which is a common weakness is novice writers' work. Instead, choose one PoV approach and stick with it.

FURTHER STUDIES

If you want to learn techniques for immersing the reader in the MC's perspective, my book *Writing Deep Point of View* teaches many advanced techniques.

For a broader overview, *Character and Viewpoint* by Orson Scott Card may be useful.

ASSIGNMENT

Choose the PoV approach you want to use: Single Limited, Serial Limited or Omniscient.

If you choose Serial Limited, decide which characters will be the temporary PoV in which scenes.

CHAPTER 14

TRUST NO ONE: SUSPICION, RESENTMENT AND BETRAYAL

In Gothic Fiction, the MC doesn't know whom she can trust. She wants to trust someone, needs to trust someone… but whom?

The people she likes turn out to be evil villains, and the people she feared are revealed as having her best interests at heart.

Indeed, sometimes the question about whom she can trust provides multiple plot twists. At the beginning of the story, she really likes someone. A third into the book, she realises that he is an evil villain. Then at the story's climax, he is revealed to be a good guy after all… And vice versa. The bad guy turns out to be good and then bad after all.

People who seem to support her may really serve the enemy's interest, or they may switch allegiance and betray her (out of greed, passion or fear) just when she needs them most. Everyone is a potential traitor, even the friend she's known from childhood, even the man she loves. The doctor, the priest, the notary and other professionals whom she trusts may be corrupt.

The worst is, she doesn't know whom to trust, and therefore is suspicious of everyone. Someone is loyal to her... but she doesn't know it. She can't risk giving her trust. Those who truly have her best interests at heart feel hurt by her distrust, and consequently withdraw.

Not knowing whom she can trust puts the MC in a very vulnerable position. Make the most of this.

THE LOVE INTEREST

In most Romance novels, it's clear from Chapter 1 who will be the MC's true love, and the reader knows that this man is trustworthy. Although the MC herself may realise his worth only gradually, the reader is sure that he's the one. In Gothic Fiction, this is less predictable.

The Love Interest may not be deserving of trust at all. He may be an evil villain who has schemed the MC's downfall. He may try to marry the MC although he has a wife already, locked up in the attic of the Gloomy House (have you read *Jane Eyre* yet?), or he may dump her to marry a wealthy heiress instead. He could also turn out to be a sexual sadist, the MC's own brother, or long dead. In Gothic Fiction, every twist is possible – the more shocking, the better.

In many Gothic novels, three men compete for the MC's hand – perhaps the charismatic owner of the Gloomy House, the handsome doctor, and her worthy but dull-seeming childhood friend. Only at the novel's climax does it become clear who is the right one for her, and it can be any of them.

In traditional Romance, the reader knows from the start whom the MC will marry, and the story lies in how the two will get together. When you blend Gothic and Romance, the story is unpredictable.

If there's just one potential Love Interest, keep the suspense high by leaving the reader in doubt about his allegiance. Let's say he's the Semi-Outsider, cousin and presumptive heir to the Sickly Invalid owner of Gloomy House. At first, they dislike each other – he believes she's trying to marry the invalid for his money, and she resents his insinuations. Then she observes his compassion towards helpless people, and believes she can trust him. But when she realises that he has revealed her secret to the lawyer, she no longer trusts. Just when she thinks of him as the enemy, he saves her life, and she trusts again. But someone is poisoning the old invalid, and this man is the only person with means, motive and opportunity. She distrusts... and so on. You can twist this as many times as you like, as long as you convince the reader every time.

During the novel's climax, the MC may realise that the Love Interest was on her side all the time, and gladly accept his proposal of marriage. But she might also discover that her dull-seeming childhood friend has hidden depths and is the dependable kind of man with whom she wants to spend her life.

She may even decide to accept the repentant villain, or to forgive the bigamist who tried to wed her while he kept his first wife locked up in the attic, like Jane Eyre whose story concludes with "Reader, I married him."

PROFESSIONAL TIP

If you want to give the MC a supporter she can trust, let it be the Outside Ally whom she has known long before she became embroiled in the affairs of the Gloomy House.

WHAT NOT TO DO

Don't make any part of the plot predictable by immediately revealing which characters are trustworthy and which are not.

ASSIGNMENT

Make a list of all the characters. Decide who is on the MC's side, and who is against her. Now think of ways to obscure this. Which character hides his true allegiance, why and how? Which character switches sides, when and why?

In a short story, one or two character twists may be enough, but in a novel, you can pile them on – and don't hesitate to make them shocking.

CHAPTER 15

ARRIVAL AT THE GLOOMY HOUSE: TOO LATE TO TURN BACK

Earlier, we discussed how almost every work of Gothic Fiction has a Gloomy House of some kind where the story unfolds. You chose and 'designed' a suitable building in the chapter 'The Gloomy Old House: Enter the Lair of Secrets'. Now let's write the scene in which the MC, an outsider, arrives to take up residence.

This is a crucial scene, introducing the location and new characters, conveying world-building, revealing new aspects of the MC's personality and immersing the reader in the atmosphere.

If you write a short story, this is probably the first scene that opens the tale. In a novel, it's often the first scene of Chapter 2.

In some novels, the arrival at the Gloomy House spreads over two scenes.

WHAT HAPPENS?

The MC arrives and sees the house from the outside for the first time. Since the reader sees it for the first time, too, spend some time on descriptions.

1. First, she sees the facade.

Show the house at a specific time of the day, in a specific season, in specific weather. This makes it 'real' to the reader and is far more interesting than a generic description. For example, a winter night with heavy snowfall creates a different atmosphere than howling winds with whirling autumn leaves at dusk or the sweltering heat of a windless summer afternoon.

Consider timing the arrival at sunset. This ticks off another trope of Gothic Fiction and allows you to create a strong atmosphere with vivid colours. It will feel right to the reader, too, because afternoon or early evening is a natural time for travellers to arrive after a long journey. (For more tips about how to write about sunsets, see the chapter 'Twilight: Moody Moments between Light and Darkness'.

Describe the facade with its colours and shapes, and add details like any cracks or signs of decay and gloom.

You may want to mention plants – the ivy clinging to the walls, the gnarled fruit trees that haven't been pruned for years, the poplars lashing like whips in the wind, the thorny brambles snaking across the path.

Describe the house in an intense but ambivalent way, to reflect the MC's intense but ambivalent emotions. On the one hand, with her conscious mind she's glad to have arrived at the house that's going to be (so she thinks) her shelter and salvation. On the other hand, her subconscious has already noticed that something is off, so she has misgivings. With the description, you can plant this in the reader's subconscious mind, too.

Similes work great here. Use a simile to compare something the MC sees with something from her background. This not only conveys the image, but it tells the reader something about the MC's background.

2. She enters through the door.

This is the moment to create suspense. Delay her on the threshold, drawing out that suspenseful moment. Perhaps she needs to search for her keys, or there's a wait until someone answers the door. Describe what she sees and hears as she waits… the flaking paint on the door, the rattling of a key chain inside. Describe the sound as the door opens.

3. She meets a character.

This meeting may take place before she reaches the door (the host waits for her outside), at the door (the parlourmaid opens), or after she's entered (she has the key, lets herself in and goes straight to the invalid in his bed).

The character may be the master/owner of the house, or the Loyal Servant. If possible, make the first character she meets someone who later plays a role in the plot.

Describe how that character moves – quietly, assertively, briskly, furtively? Describe what her voice sounds like. Also show something about her face and clothes – not a comprehensive description, just a couple of telling details. Is the lace apron as white as baking flour and neatly starched, or is it crinkled and smudged? Is the blouse buttoned up wrongly, are the sleeves rolled up? Are the earrings crucifixes, gilded cannabis leaves or Christmas baubles?

Use the dialogue to establish that character's job, as well as his attitude to his job and to the new arrival. Is he efficient, resentful, relieved, respectful, curious…?

3. The character sees a room (or two) of the house.

Probably that other character takes her there. Which room is it? Her bedroom? The master's study? The parlour? The dining room? The nursery?

What does she do there? What does she observe?

Describe smells indoors. What does the house smell of inside? What does her bedroom smell of? Smells pull the reader into the experience.

Once inside the Gloomy House, perhaps in the room or on the way there, the MC may notice something that's a bit weird. It could be another person running past, or the sound of footsteps above the ceiling when allegedly the attic is locked and never used, or maybe an incongruous painting at the top of the staircase. She doesn't dwell on the oddity, because she has more important things on her mind, but her subconscious registers it. Mention it in passing, so the reader's subconscious registers it, too. You can pick it up again later, when the MC compares it with other clues.

EXAMPLES FROM LITERATURE

Jane Eyre, by Charlotte Bronte

We now slowly ascended a drive, and came upon the long front of a house: candlelight gleamed from one curtained bow-window; all the rest were dark.

Cousin Kate, by Georgette Heyer

Kate's first view of the great house drew a gasp from her, not of admiration but of dismay, since it seemed to her for a moment, staring at the huge facade, whose numberless windows gave back the sun's dying rays in every colour of the spectrum, that the building was on fire.

PROFESSIONAL TIP

Plant small hints about the MC's background by weaving them into the plot. For example, when you show her enjoying the soft pillows and lavender-scented sheets of her bed, you can add how glad she is to relax in a real bed again after all those years of sleeping on the floor. When she closes her bedroom door, you can mention what a difference this is to sharing a dormitory with six other destitute actresses. But keep those mini-hints short – just a sentence at a time, and not many of them.

WHAT NOT TO DO

Don't describe the journey there. (The journey to the destination tends to be boring for readers, and they tend to skip it, so you may just as well save yourself the work of writing it.)

Don't use flashbacks, memories or summaries of what happened in the past. Focus fully on what happens now.

FURTHER STUDIES

My book *Writing Vivid Settings* can help you write a vivid description of the Gloomy House.

ASSIGNMENT

Write a first draft for this scene. It can be very rough. Just get it written – you can revise and refine it later.

CHAPTER 16

THE DOOR OF THE DOOMED: HEIGHTENING SUSPENSE

My favourite technique for increasing suspense works supremely well in Gothic Fiction: let your protagonist walk through a doorway on her way to danger.

I call this the 'Bluebeard Effect' after the frightening fairy tale. If you haven't read it, you should – it's a distinctly Gothic story, with many of the Gothic tropes. Several versions are available free to read online.

Subconsciously, the viewer perceives the door as a barrier: if the MC crosses this threshold, she is entering a danger zone. The viewer screams inwardly, "Don't open that door!" Of course, the MC opens it and enters. By now, the reader sits on the edge of her chair, frightened on the MC's behalf, needing to find out what happens next.

Whenever you plan a particularly exciting scene, put a door between your MC and the danger, and linger for a moment before she or he enters.

If you're writing a novel and using the Hero's Journey plot model, use a door or gate to mark the 'Crossing the Threshold' point.

TWO OPPORTUNITIES TO USE THIS TECHNIQUE

We've already looked at this technique briefly for the scene in which the MC arrives at the Gloomy House. Here are some ideas how you can flesh the moment out further:

Whether the MC unlocks it herself, or gets bowed in by a butler, find a way to slow the action and delay the entry. Perhaps she can't immediately find the keys, or the lock is stuck, or maybe there's a wait before the parlourmaid comes to the door, or the butler refuses to let her in.

Describe the door – the dust-streaked glass pane, the peeling black paint revealing streaks of crimson underneath, the ivy clinging to the door jamb, the cracked threshold. Are there any danger clues, such as knife marks, smashed glass, ominous stains, thorny plants, perhaps even a sign "Visitors Unwelcome" or "Keep Out" nailed to the centre?

Add sounds – the banging of the big door knocker, the approach of footsteps from inside, the rattling of the door chain, the creaking of the hinges when the door finally opens, the high-pitched voice of the parlourmaid.

The sense of temperature can often give additional descriptions: does the doorknob feel icy in the MC's palm? Does the bunch of keys feel heavy in her hand? Does a wave of thick warm air waft into her face on entering?

The second opportunity is when the MC enters a room where the real danger waits… perhaps the underground chamber, the attic, the Greedy Villain's study, the Obsessed Scientist's laboratory or the crypt where the vampire sleeps.

Again, delay the MC on the threshold. Let her hesitate, have second thoughts. Maybe she listens at the door for a while and only enters when she's almost sure that nobody is inside. Again, describe what the door looks like and how it sounds. Does it creak open or screech open? Does it rattle or whisper? Does it whine inwards on its hinges? The sense of smell is useful for this 'crossing the threshold' experience. Let the MC perceive the smell of the place the moment she enters.

By the time your protagonist steps through the door, the reader's suspense is turned to high volume, intensely anticipating what happens next.

EXAMPLES FROM LITERATURE

Rebecca by Daphne du Maurier

Here's the famous opening of this novel:

Last night I dreamt I went to Manderley again. It seemed to me I stood by the iron gate leading to the drive, and for a while I could not enter, for the way was barred to me. There was a padlock and a chain upon the gate. I called in my dream to the lodge-keeper, and had no answer, and peering closer through the rusted spokes of the gate I saw that the lodge was uninhabited.

Jane Eyre, by Charlotte Bronte

I followed still, up a very narrow staircase to the attics, and thence by a ladder and through a trap-door to the roof of the hall.

I was now on a level with the crow colony, and could see into their nests. Leaning over the battlements and looking far down, I surveyed the grounds laid out like a map: the bright and velvet lawn closely girdling the grey base of the mansion; the field, wide as a park, dotted with its ancient timber; the wood, dun and sere, divided by a path visibly overgrown, greener with moss than the trees were with foliage; the church at the gates, the road, the tranquil hills, all reposing in the autumn day's sun; the horizon bounded by a propitious sky, azure, marbled with pearly white. No feature in the scene was extraordinary, but all was pleasing.

When I turned from it and repassed the trap-door, I could scarcely see my way down the ladder; the attic seemed black as a vault compared with that arch of blue air to which I had been looking up, and to that sunlit scene of grove, pasture, and green hill, of which the hall was the centre, and over which I had been gazing with delight. Mrs. Fairfax stayed behind a moment to fasten the trap-door; I, by dint of groping, found the outlet from the attic, and proceeded to descend the narrow garret staircase.

I lingered in the long passage to which this led, separating the front and back rooms of the third storey: narrow, low, and dim, with only one little window at the far end, and looking, with its two rows of small black doors all shut, like a corridor in some Bluebeard's castle.

PROFESSIONAL TIP

If you want to increase the suspense further still, describe the sound of the door as it closes behind her.

The door snapped shut.

Behind her, the door groaned shut.

The door thudded closed.

The door clanked into its lock.

This suggests that the protagonist has just walked into a trap, and that her escape route is blocked. Now the reader will be super-excited.

WHAT NOT TO DO

This technique builds up expectations, so use it only if something exciting happens inside. Don't use it if the MC merely goes to the kitchen for a chat with the cook, or into her bedroom where she enjoys a night of undisturbed sleep.

FURTHER STUDIES

My book *Writing Scary Scenes* in the Writer's Craft series contains many more techniques for arousing suspense and fear in the reader.

ASSIGNMENT

Choose a moment when the MC is about to enter a danger zone.

This could be on her arrival at the Gloomy House. For this, you may revise a section of the scene you've already drafted.

Alternatively, choose the door leading to the villain's inner sanctum, or some other dangerous place.

Describe what how the door looks and opens. After the MC has entered, the door closes behind her.

I suggest you use 30-200 words for this.

CHAPTER 17

STORMY WEATHER: PAINT A DRAMATIC BACKGROUND

Setting a scene in windy and stormy weather increases the excitement and drama, and Gothic Fiction uses this technique a lot.

Whether the scene unfolds on windswept moors, on a windswept hilltop, in a windswept cemetery, on a windswept beach... let it be windy. Or better still, escalate the breeze to a storm.

WHAT KIND OF STORM?

For plausibility, research what type of storms occur in that region and in what month. For example, when I lived in South East England, October always brought several intense storms, and some of those were fierce: uprooting trees; damaging buildings; disrupting traffic. So for a novel set in South East England, a ferocious October storm would be a great choice.

During my childhood on the shores of Lake Constance in the south of Germany, we often got föhn, a warm, dry wind sweeping down from the Alps. The föhn didn't cause physical damages, but it affected the human body and emotions. The tension in the air was palpable, and it affected the mind. Many people experienced headaches (piercing in one eye and hammering across half the skull) or an aggravation of existing heart problems – and quite a few suffered from irritability and irrational nervousness. For a story set in that region, a character affected by the föhn – whether the villain, the Helpless Invalid, or the MC herself – would be believable and enrich the plot.

Use whatever wind or storm is plausible in that geographical area: wind with or without rain, hail, thunder and lighting, a stiff sea breeze, a blizzard, a tornado or a hurricane.

To add excitement, let the storm happen either earlier in the year than expected, or make it more ferocious than usual. This ensures that characters are not fully prepared for the onslaught.

WHEN DOES THE STORM ARISE?

You can insert the storm to support any scene you like. Here are several moments when it works especially well:

- The MC's arrival at the Gloomy House. (Perhaps she didn't seek out this destination, but is forced by the unexpected storm to seek shelter.)

- A love scene. If they're outdoors and a storm rages around them, the scene won't suffer from over-sweet sentimentality but will gain dramatic impact.

- Indoors, waiting for something. The MC awaits the arrival of an important character or a paranormal/supernatural manifestation.

- Captivity. The MC is newly locked up in her bed chamber or in the attic.

- Escape. The MC flees from the Gloomy House... but, unaware of weather patterns in this region, she gets caught in a storm that's almost impossible to survive out of doors.

- Climax. A storm adds intense excitement to a story's climax scene.

- The destruction of the Gloomy House. Some types of storms can demolish buildings.

- Before the destruction of the Gloomy House. The storm may damage the house, so it becomes vulnerable to the disaster that strikes soon after. Some types of storm actually bring disasters in their wake – for example, some storms are commonly followed by floods or fires.

You can extend the storm over several scenes – assuming that it's a type of storm that doesn't blow itself out in a couple of hours. In this case, let it start slowly and build in intensity.

USING THE SENSES

Indulge in sensory descriptions.

Show the visual effects – whether it's flower petals or autumn leaves raining down from the trees, whole branches falling or tree trunks getting uprooted, plastic bags and soda bottles racing along asphalted pavements, giant waves building like walls on the sea and collapsing into heaps of foam, tree saplings bending flat under the force or vehicles overturning. Describe the sky: clouds racing, lightning flashes zigzagging and more.

Activate the sense of touch – what the MC feels on her skin – if she's out-of-doors. The icy wind stings her cheeks, the dust storm clogs her nostrils and eyes, or she needs to lean diagonally into the wind in order to walk forward. The same applies to the sense of temperature. Let the MC feel the effects as the temperature changes gradually.

Above all, use noises. There may be a deafening howl, a soft rustle building into roar, a whistle as the storm approaches. Branches creak under the wind's force and scrape against buildings. Objects clatter as they race along the paths and bang into walls. The thunder may sound like it scratches, tears or rolls across the sky. Loose roof tiles fall to the ground and shatter. Indoors, the character may hear window shutters and unsecured doors rattle, gusts slapping against walls, tree branches scraping the roof, hail hammering at the windowpanes and wind whining in the chimney.

HOW DO ANIMALS REACT?

Animals often sense the approaching storm before humans do. You can use this effect to build suspense. Songbirds cease their chirping, swallows fly low, farm animals turn their back to the wind and some pets hide in small spaces. Dogs – with a sense of hearing many times better than that of a human – may first alert the MC and the reader – that something is wrong. If your story has the Dog as a character, he may bark, whine, pace, sniff, pace, drool and spin.

During the storm, if animals are present, show their reaction. Research this, so their behaviour is appropriate for the species. Do they hide, cower, whine, shake in fear, or just curl up in a cardboard box for a nap?

EXAMPLES FROM LITERATURE

Wuthering Heights, by Emily Bronte

About midnight, while we still sat up, the storm came rattling over the Heights in full fury. There was a violent wind, as well as thunder, and either one or the other split a tree off at the corner of the building: a huge bough fell across the roof, and knocked down a portion of the east chimney-stack, sending a clatter of stones and soot into the kitchen-fire.

The Fall of the House of Usher, by Edgar Allan Poe

Thus speaking, and having carefully shaded his lamp, he hurried to one of the casements, and threw it freely open to the storm. The impetuous fury of the entering gust nearly lifted us from our feet. It was, indeed, a tempestuous yet sternly beautiful night, and one wildly singular in its terror and its beauty. A whirlwind had apparently collected its force in our vicinity; for there were frequent and violent alterations in the direction of the wind; and the exceeding density of the clouds (which hung so low as to press upon the turrets of the house) did not prevent our perceiving the life-like velocity with which they flew careering from all points against each other, without passing away into the distance.

The Gabriel Hounds, by Mary Stewart

I'm not sure whether it was the flash of lightning or the almost simultaneous crack of thunder that woke me, but as I stirred in bed and opened my eyes the sound of rain seemed to obliterate all else. I have never heard such rain. There was no wind with it, only the cracking of thunder and the vivid white rents in the black sky. I sat up in bed to watch. The window-arches flickered dramatically against the storm outside, and the portcullis squares of the grille stamped themselves on the room over and over again with their violently angled perspectives of black and white. Through the window that I had opened the scents of flowers came almost storming in, vividly wakened by the rain. With the scents came, more palpably, a good deal of the rain itself, hitting the sill and splashing on the floor in great hammering drops.

Touch Not the Cat, by Mary Stewart

A sound came, breaking through the very thought, shattering it. A cracking, creaking noise, like a big door strained to breaking point. The noise was drowned by a lashing gust of wind, then in the lull behind the wind it came again.

PROFESSIONAL TIP

Make the most of sounds. Sound effects are the magic ingredients for this scene, guaranteeing excitement.

WHAT NOT TO DO

Don't just state that the weather is windy or that there's a storm raging. Describe the effects.

FURTHER STUDY

My book *Writing Vivid Settings* contains many techniques for using the weather in fiction.

ASSIGNMENT

1. Decide on the scene which will feature a heavy wind of some kind.

2. Now choose the location (is the MC indoors or out of doors?) and the type of wind (stiff breeze or hurricane? Hailstorm or föhn?).

3. Make a list of storm-related sounds the MC will hear in her location. Try to think of at least ten. Coming up with so many may be a challenge, but it will be worth the effort.

CHAPTER 18

TWILIGHT: MOODY MOMENTS BETWEEN LIGHT AND DARKNESS

Try to set at least one of your scenes during dawn (sunrise) or dusk (sunset), because twilight is very Gothic. The transition between night and day reflects the crossing of other boundaries in Gothic Fiction, such as between present and past, or life and death.

Twilight scenes are visually exciting, with spectacular colour effects. Use your creativity to describe the sight.

WHAT TO DESCRIBE

While the changing colours on the horizon – yellow, orange, pink, lilac, purple and more – are the most spectacular feature, a lot more goes on.

As the sun moves towards the horizon in the evening, shadows lengthen. The characters' bodies may throw long shadows, many times their actual length. Often, everything appears to be dipped into a warm golden glow. The temperature drops noticeably the further the sun sinks. Some flowers close towards evening, folding their petals further in the more the sun sinks. Depending on the geographic location, there may be increased birdsong towards the end of the day which ceases the moment the sun has sunk, creating an eerie silence. Some insect activity increases before or after sunset.

As the sun rises, the animal world wakes up. There may be cocks crowing (even before the sun is up) and birds twittering in a dawn chorus. When describing dawn, watch the effect on the ground –

e.g. the frost-rimmed grasses shimmering, the night frost gradually receding except close to the walls, dew drops evaporating from the lawn, flowers opening their petals to the sun. Also consider the noises humans make: shopkeepers opening their rattling shutters, cars vrooming past taking commuters to work.

When I lived on the coast in England, pre-dawn brought the distant cries of seagulls. The gulls weren't responding to the sunrise itself, but were trailing the pre-dawn fishing fleet and snatching discarded fish. Here in rural Bulgaria, I always hear the tinkling of goats' bells soon after sunrise and shortly before dusk, as the local goatherd takes the animals to pasture and leads them back home.

CONSIDER THE LOCATION, THE SEASON AND THE WEATHER

Sunset and sunrise occur at different times of the day depending on the season and the location. Do some research – you can find this information online – so you won't have the sun sink at 15.00 when it should be 21.00.

The location also decides whether your MC can see a sunrise or a sunset, or both, or neither. The sun rises in the east and sinks in the west. You may want to draw a sketch map of the setting, including the Gloomy House, so you know if the MC can really see a sunrise from her bedroom window, or if there's a mountain range blocking the view.

The weather plays a big role, too. Sunrises and sunsets look different depending on whether the air is warm, cold, misty or dry. A few clouds can add dramatic patterns, but if the sky is overcast, you will see little if any colour effects. Stormy weather and rain wipe out the gorgeous sunset colours, so use 'stormy weather' and 'twilight' in different scenes.

So definitely do some research, by checking facts online, by asking local people for descriptions, and where possible, by visiting the place in person.

EXAMPLES FROM LITERATURE

Wuthering Heights by Emily Bronte

A sorrowful sight I saw: dark night coming down prematurely, and sky and hills mingled in one bitter whirl of wind and suffocating snow.

Nine Coaches Waiting, by Mary Stewart

Outside the dusk fell rapidly; the windows were oblongs of murky grey.

The Strange Case of Dr Jekyll and Mr Hyde, by Robert Louis Stephenson

It was by this time about nine in the morning, and the first fog of the season. A great chocolate-coloured pall lowered over heaven, but the wind was continually charging and routing these embattled vapours, so that as the cab crawled from street to street, Mr Utterson beheld a marvellous number of degrees and hues of twilight; for here it would be dark like the back-end of evening; and there would be a glow of rich, lurid brown, like the light of some strange conflagration; and here, for a moment, the fog would be quite broken up, and a haggard shaft of daylight would glance in between the swirling wreaths.

Touch Not the Cat, by Mary Stewart

It was dusk already. As I stood there the sun, imperceptibly, withdrew, and the light cooled to blue and then to shadow.

The Reluctant Widow, by Georgette Heyer

It was dusk when the London to Little Hampton stagecoach lurched into the village of Billingshurst, and a cold mist was beginning to creep knee-high over the dimly seen countryside.

PROFESSIONAL TIP

Although sunsets are generally romantic to look at, you can insert a note of foreboding by choosing 'ominous' vocabulary. For example, you may describe the purple bruises in the sky or the crimson slashes on the horizon as the day bleeds into night.

If you can, go outside and experience sunsets and sunrises in the environment where the story takes place.

Look at photos, watch videos.

Sunsets and sunrises look different from region to region, at different times of the year, and in different weather.

Make sure you get it right – for the location, the season and the weather. Above all, check what the character can actually see.

The sun rises in the east and sinks in the west. You need to be consistent. If the sun rises on one side of the Gloomy House, it can 't sink on that side again. Depending on the location, the MC may not be able to see the colourful spectacle at all. If the house stands on a mountain slope, that mountain may block the view of the sunrise or sunset.

WHAT NOT TO DO

Don't just write detailed descriptions of sunsets and sunrises. Something has to happen in that scene; the sunset and sunrise is merely the colourful backdrop.

Don't undermine your story's plausibility by placing a sunset or sunrise in the wrong direction or at the wrong time.

I once read a Gothic Historical Romance where the heroine stood on the White Cliffs of Dover, gazing across the sea at the sinking sun. Ahem! The White Cliffs of Dover are on England's eastern coast. Standing above the cliffs gazing across the sea, the heroine might have seen the coast of France and – in the morning – the rising sun. But she definitely wouldn't have seen the sun set in that direction. I know, because at the time I lived nearby. After that blunder, I couldn't believe in the novel's historical accuracy or the characters' emotions anymore, and I didn't buy another book by that author.

FURTHER STUDIES

Writing Vivid Settings in the Writer's Craft series shows techniques for describing indoor and outdoor locations during the daytime and at night.

ASSIGNMENT

Go outside and experience either a sunset or a sunrise. Take notes about sounds, colours, atmosphere, temperature and more. Describe the experience creatively, to weave into a scene later.

(When you use it, you may need to adapt it to suit the season and location.)

CHAPTER 19

CAPTIVITY SCENES: LOCKED UP AND SCHEMING

Many Gothic stories involve a prisoner. A person is locked up somewhere in the Gloomy House – probably in the underground chamber or in the attic. He may also be imprisoned in his own bedroom, especially if he's the Sickly Invalid, the Helpless Child or the Mentally Deranged Person. Sometimes the MC herself is held captive.

Most (not all) Gothic novels have a captivity scene, but many short stories don't. So if there's nobody held captive in your story, you can skip this chapter's assignment.

FROM THE CAPTIVE'S POINT OF VIEW

If the MC herself gets locked up – perhaps because the villain is obsessively in love with her and wants to force her to become his bride, or he tries to make her submit to his deviant carnal desires – then write the scene from her PoV.

Here are some tips.

1. Describe the sound as the cell door closes. Does it clank, screech or thud shut? Let the reader hear the related noises as well, such as rattling of keys in the lock and the thudding of boots as the jailer (the villain himself, or the Loyal Retainer) walks away.

2. If possible, make the room dark or semi-dark. This is creepier than daylight and can be unnerving for the reader as well as the

character. If she's imprisoned in a windowless underground chamber, you can make the darkness almost absolute. The attic could also be windowless, or perhaps have just a small one in the roof. If she's imprisoned in luxury, perhaps in a comfortable bedchamber, perhaps the villain has had the windows boarded up, so she can't signal for help. Whatever the situation, emphasise the scarcity of light: the narrow rectangle of light falling through the high up window slit; the flickering torch; the faint illumination from the moon.

3. During the character's first moments in the cell, describe what the place smells like. Olfactory impressions are strongest at the beginning. After a while, the mind gets used to them and they are no longer noticeable, so mention the stinks when the character notices them, which is the moment she enters that room.

    If she's locked up in a dungeon where other prisoners were kept before her, the smells may be seriously unpleasant: the sour stench of urine, excrement from previous prisoners, old sweat, blood, rodent excrement, rotten straw, mould.

    In an attic normally used for storage, there may be smells of must, dust (that's not really a smell as such, but she'll perceive it in her nostrils), rat excrement, mothballs.

    If she's imprisoned in a comfortable room, the smells may be pleasant – but by emphasising them, you can convey an intense experience that creates an ominous effect. Consider the smells of furniture treatment and cleaning materials (beeswax furniture polish or synthetic cleaner), mothballs, soap, coal smoke (or smells from whatever is used to heat the place), the contents of the chamber pot (especially if it doesn't have a lid).

    If she's imprisoned in the room where she's already stayed the previous night, she won't notice smells, so you can skip this part.

4. In Gothic Fiction, she's probably the only prisoner. This means solitary confinement, which is scary. If your character is alone in that room, with nobody to talk to, the reader worries for her. The MC may shout, "Is anyone out there? Can you hear me?" and bang on walls and doors without getting a reply.

   Alternatively, she may have a companion in her captivity – until that person gets taken away. If several people are confined in a closed space, describe body odours, movements, overheard snatches of conversation, snores, habits.

5. The room is probably cold, especially if it's in the underground chamber or the attic in the winter, and you may want to make it very chilly indeed. Perhaps the place is unheated, the protagonist is not wearing many clothes, the air is chilly, the concrete floor is cold, and the blanket – if one is provided at all – is much too thin.

6. Use sounds. Sounds create unease and fear in the reader's subconscious – perfect for this type of scene. Here are some ideas: clanking doors, rattling keys, screeching locks, thudding boots or clicking heels in the corridor, rodents' feet, shuffling straw, fellow captives' sobs and snores, agonised screams from another room (if the villain uses torture or experiments on humans), innocuous noises coming from outside (car motors, rattling carriage wheels, the Dog barking, the waves crashing against the rocky shore, and the wind whispering or howling).

   If the cell is underground, innocuous outside noises may not be heard.

7. Mention how something feels to the touch. This works especially well if the place is dark.

   In an underground dungeon, she may feel the fetters/handcuffs/bonds chafing at the wrists/ankles, pain from bruises, the texture of the wall, the texture of the door, the cold hard floor, the rough blanket, cobwebs, sodden straw, chilly air.

If she's imprisoned in the attic, she'll probably feel the signs of dereliction and decay – rotten window frames, loose roof tiles, crumbling walls and such. These may actually give her hope, because she may be able to break out.

On the other hand, if she's being held prisoner in a comfortable bedroom, she may feel the cool smooth satin of the bed sheets and the softness of the fleece rug beneath her bare feet.

8. Perhaps you can involve the sense of taste as well. What does the food taste like? The water? However, this may not be appropriate for all captivity scenes. The perception of taste also depends on how hungry and thirsty the prisoner is. At first, she may find the gruel and brackish water revolting, but after a while, she's so starved and parched, she'll devour and swallow what she can get.

If the villain has gagged the MC, you can also describe how the gag tastes.

9. The captive examines the place, looking for ways to escape. This is a natural response to captivity, especially during the first few hours. It's also a good way to show the reader how secure the prison is. Describe how strong the wall is, how high up and narrow the windows are placed and how several locks secure the door, with two jailers standing guard.

10. The jail guard – who brings her food, empties the slop bucket and checks up on her – is probably the Loyal Retainer, the one who is fanatically loyal to the master. He may refuse to engage in any conversation.

11. The pace in captivity scenes is slow, because the character is condemned to inactivity. Use this part of your novel to share the character's thoughts with the reader. She may reflect on her mistakes, gain insights and grow wiser. But don't allow the character to wallow in despair. Although she may feel dejected, she doesn't give up.

12. The MC has a sliver of hope that she might escape. This hope keeps the tension alive. Let her hope and plan. Later, the plan may succeed or fail, but it's important to show some hope in order to create suspense.

13. The captive plots and schemes. In her cell, she has plenty of time to think, and she uses those insights to plan her next steps.

FROM THE VISITOR'S POINT OF VIEW

In Gothic Fiction, the prisoner may be someone other than the MC – perhaps it's the Love Interest, the Helpless Child or the Naive Bride.

Perhaps the MC knows there's a prisoner in the house, and schemes to visit or rescue him. Perhaps she discovers the prisoner by accident, while looking for something else. Or maybe the prisoner managed to attract her attention somehow, by knocking on the floor or by waving curtains in Morse code.

If the MC is visiting the captive in prison, or rescuing him from his confinement, her immediate attention won't be on the place, but on the person of the captive. Does he look pale or healthy? Emaciated or strong? Does his voice sound feeble, dejected or defiant?

She will take in the surroundings, but not in great depth, because unlike the prisoner, the visitor doesn't have the time. Indeed, she may be in a great hurry, because any moment the jailer (the Obsessed Scientist, Corrupt Doctor, Corrupt Priest or Loyal Retainer) may come.

She will notice the smells the moment she enters the cell. Other senses will come into play as well, but only briefly.

FROM THE JAILER'S POINT OF VIEW

This is the least likely option in Gothic Fiction, but not impossible. Perhaps you're writing the story (or this particular scene) from the PoV of the Greedy Villain, Corrupt Doctor, Obsessed Scientist, Loyal Retainer or whoever holds the victim captive. Or perhaps the good guy has locked up one of the evil-doers until the police arrives.

Either way, the jailer will observe the captive more than the place.

The place is familiar to him, so he no longer pays much attention. He's unlikely to notice the accustomed smells and noises.

However, he'll observe the prisoner, and his interest is similar to that of a visitor: how healthy, strong, emaciated, pale is she? His interest is probably not compassionate, but related to his intentions. A kidnapper needs his victim in good health, while a torturer assesses her capability to suffer and stay alive, while the Obsessed Scientist engaged in human experiments and the Corrupt Doctor driving his victim insane will carefully observe and record every change.

He'll closely listen to the sound of her voice, to detect any note of dejection, despair, rebellion or defiance.

In addition, he'll double-check the security features – the manacles on her wrists, bars on the windows, the door locks.

EXAMPLES FROM LITERATURE

Cousin Kate, by Georgette Heyer

She winced as the thunder crashed again, but slid out of her bed, and caught up her shawl. Hastily wrapping this round herself, she groped her way to the door, intending to open it, so that she could hear more clearly. She cautiously turned the handle, but the door remained shut. She had been locked in.

In unreasoning panic she tugged at the handle, and beat with clenched fists on the panels. The noise was drowned by another clap of thunder, which drove her back to her bed, blundering into the furniture, and feeling blindly for the table which stood beside it. Her fingers at last found the tinder-box, but they were trembling so much that it was some time before she succeeded in striking the spark. She relit her candle, but even as the little tongue of flame dimly illuminated the room, her panic abated, and was succeeded by anger. She climbed into bed again, and sat hugging her knees, trying to find the answer to two insoluble problems: who had locked her in, and why?

The Castle of Otranto, by Horace Walpole

Manfred thus saw his commands even cheerfully obeyed; and appointing a guard, with strict orders to prevent any food being conveyed to the prisoner, he dismissed his friends and attendants, and retired to his own chamber, after locking the gates of the castle in which he suffered none but his domestics to remain.

The Gabriel Hounds, by Mary Stewart

I opened blurred eyes on a dark wall where shadows moved slightly like rags in a draught. It was warm and very quiet, a heavy airless quiet that slowly conveyed to me the sense of being shut in.

PROFESSIONAL TIP

The captivity scene (especially if the MC is the prisoner) works well for the Black Moment of a novel.

Some Gothic novels have two captivity scenes. The first time the MC may be held prisoner in relative comfort, because the villain still hopes that she will give in to his demands (for marriage, sex, or whatever), but the second time, the captivity serves as punishment, and she's allowed no luxury and suffers harsh treatment.

WHAT NOT TO DO

A mistake inexperienced writers make is to rely overly on visual descriptions and miss out the powerful senses of sound, touch and smell.

FURTHER STUDIES

Some of this chapter's content overlaps with a chapter in my book *Writing Vivid Scenes,* which also contains advice on crafting fight scenes, love scenes, erotic scenes, argument scenes and more.

ASSIGNMENTS

(You can skip these if your story involves no captivity.)

1. Write three sentences describing sounds, to insert into different parts of the scene.

2. Write one sentence each based on the following senses: touch, temperature, smell.

3. Write a rough draft for this scene. This can be a very rough draft.

CHAPTER 20

ESCAPE SCENES: RUN FOR YOUR LIFE

Does your MC escape from the dungeon/attic/bedchamber or whatever room she was locked up in? Maybe she's running away from the Gloomy House?

Part of the escape probably takes place indoors, part outdoors.

Here are some techniques to make your chase scene exciting.

POINT OF VIEW

Unless you've chosen omniscient PoV, stay in the fleeing MC's PoV throughout, showing only what she sees, hears and feels.

Show what's immediately before her. She will be looking for an escape route, a hiding place or a way to shake off her pursuer, so she'll notice alleyways, rubbish skips, cellar entrances and the like. But she won't pause to think about the architectural styles or the design of the flowerbeds on the way. (On the other hand, she may recognise features she's observed before. For example, that big staircase, that broken window, that dilapidated tool shed.)

While the MC runs for her life, she won't pause to watch her pursuer, so don't describe what the pursuer looks like, or how the distance between gradually closes. However, you can describe the sounds the pursuer makes: boots thudding on the asphalt coming closer and closer, clanking armour, yells, curses.

PACING

Chases are fast-paced, so use fast-paced writing techniques: short paragraphs, short sentences, short words. But if the chase or escape spreads over more than a few paragraphs, try to vary the pace. This will make it more exciting. When the MC character runs fast, use very short sentences – even sentence fragments – and mostly single-syllabic words. They create a sense of breathlessness and fear. When she's hiding, when she's struggling to climb up a facade inch by inch, when the pursuers have trapped her and when the policeman handcuffs her, use medium-length sentences and words.

READER SYMPATHY

Readers tend to sympathise with the fleeing person. If that's your MC, you can increase the sympathy effect if several people (and, since this is Gothic Fiction, dogs) are hounding the refugee. Nothing stirs reader emotion more than a situation of many against one.

DANGER FROM THE SURROUNDINGS

Make the most of the setting. Increase the tension by shifting the action to dangerous ground. As your heroine flees from the evil villain, she may run down a collapsing staircase or climb out of the window of the burning tower. Even as she gets away from the Gloomy House, she moves towards quicksand, a crumbling bridge, a cliff edge or a ravine.

Sometimes, the escape scene happens during the destruction of the Gloomy House. The MC flees from the flaming inferno, the walls caving in after the earthquake or the rapidly rising flood.

STUMBLING

When a person runs from danger, a cocktail of chemicals gets released in the brain. It includes adrenalin and other substances which dull pain and give stamina but also impair motor skills. Your fugitive's movements won't be as coordinated as they usually are, so she may miss her footing, stumble or slip. The likelihood of tripping is high, because in her desperate hurry, she won't examine the ground on which she's treading. Use the dereliction of the house to provide stumbling blocks. Does she stumble across poorly laid carpet edge, a loose floor tile or a missing step in the staircase?

PHYSICAL SYMPTOMS

The running characters are probably out of breath, struggling to get enough oxygen. Describe how the PoV character's chest feels like it's about to burst. Her heart thuds loudly, not only in her chest but in her head. This thudding continues even when she stops running, and while she's hiding, the heartbeat in her head may be the loudest noise she hears.

CHASES BY CAR AND ON HORSEBACK

It's possible that she gets away far enough from the Gloomy House that she can jump into a vehicle or ride an animal. In this case, the physical symptoms will be less intense, although the PoV character may still hear her heart drum with excitement or fear. Instead, focus on the noises the vehicles or animals make: screeching tyres, shrieking breaks, panting breath, hooves on asphalt.

Once the pursuer catches up with the fugitive, he'll have to stop her car (or her horse, sled or aeroplane) before he can get at her. Think about how you're going to write that. You may need to ask a professional driver, horse person, pilot or other expert for advice so the action is plausible and authentic.

BYSTANDERS

You can add interest by throwing other people into the action – people who go about their everyday business and are in the way of the fugitive or the pursuers. Don't describe them in detail (your PoV won't take time to observe them), just show how the characters interact with them. For example, your PoV character may upend a market trader's stall in order to block the pursuer's path, or the pursuer may ask, "Which direction did that woman run?" The pursuer may also hurriedly enlist the help of bystanders, e.g. "Stop that thief!" or "Follow that car!"

In a short story, keep the involvement of bystanders to a minimum or leave them out altogether.

FELLOW ESCAPEES

Does she flee together with someone else, or is she alone? Perhaps she has a companion on this adventure, and they help each other, each contributing special skills. Or perhaps she is saving a helpless character, maybe an injured victim of the villain's cruelty, or an abused small child.

Perhaps the fellow escapee gives up or gets recaptured. Or perhaps he sacrifices himself so the MC can get away. Alternatively, the MC may manage to take her vulnerable companion to safety before she herself gets caught.

THE CHASE ENDS IN A FIGHT

Does the pursuer catch the fugitive? In Gothic Fiction, he often does. Just when she thought she had reached safety, the villain recaptures her and returns her to the Gloomy House.

When the pursuer catches up with the fugitive, let her put up a fight. This moment is the Climax of the scene, so make it exciting.

BETRAYAL

Treachery and betrayal play a big role in Gothic Fiction. Perhaps someone aided the MC's escape... only to reveal her flight plans to the villain. This betrayal hurts – as do her dashed hopes.

AFTER THE ESCAPE

In the scene following the escape and recapture, the MC often finds herself back in the Gloomy House – but this time locked up in a more secure, less comfortable prison.

PROFESSIONAL TIP

Give the MC the opportunity to use her special skills for her escape. Her background, hobby or profession have given her the knowledge or skill she needs to overcome a problem during her flight. If she's an architect, she'll guess where the postern is located, and if she used to grow up among circus folk, she may have acrobatic skills and so is able to swing from one tree branch to another, high up in the forest canopy out of sight of the her pursuers.

EXAMPLE FROM LITERATURE

The Gabriel Hounds, by Mary Stewart

I hung there, irresolute, gasping, while the hounds whined and shivered and stayed close. The caravan was due soon, and presumably by the postern. But I had heard Halide say that the postern was locked and the key out of it. It would have to be the main gate, and chance it. I ran up the passage to my right, and had stumbled perhaps some twenty yards on the rough and ill-lit cobbles when Sofi whined again and I heard, clearly ahead of me, a turmoil of shouts from the main court. I stopped dead.

Nine Coaches Waiting, by Mary Stewart

I don't remember moving, but as I let go the banister I fled – was swept – up the stairway in front of him, only to check desperately on the landing and whirl to face him. I shrieked: 'Run, Philippe!' and put up frantic, futile hands to break the tempest.

WHAT NOT TO DO

Don't let the MC faint at the moment of recapture. In the early Gothic novels of the 18th and 19th century, fainting heroines were acceptable. But modern readers prefer spunky female characters, even in Historical Fiction. Her struggle can be short, lasting only for a moment while he presses the chloroform-soaked cloth on her face, but she must make an effort to resist.

FURTHER STUDY

Some of this chapter's content overlaps with a chapter in my book *Writing Vivid Scenes,* which also contains advice on crafting fight scenes, love scenes, erotic scenes, argument scenes and more.

ASSIGNMENT

1. Visualise the escape route. Where does the chase begin (probably in the house) and end (probably out of doors in a remote dangerous location)? What obstacles are in the way?

2. Now imagine the escape from the MC's PoV.

3. And finally, write a rough draft for the scene.

CHAPTER 21

DRAMATIC DEMISE: THE DESTRUCTION OF THE GLOOMY HOUSE

The old, Gloomy House that played such a big part in the tale often gets destroyed at the end.

This is a wonderfully dramatic moment, so make the most of it, with narrow escapes, dangerous rescues and spectacular visuals.

HOW DOES THE DESTRUCTION HAPPEN?

The house could burn to the ground, collapse in an earthquake, explode, disappear into a sinkhole, get washed away by a tsunami or a flood, get bombed, get knocked down by a hurricane, get carried away by a landslide or avalanche, buried under the lava stream of an erupting volcano...

Consider the setting. What kind of destruction is most plausible in this location? If the house stands in the mountains, then an avalanche is more likely than a flood. If it stands on the beach, it's more likely to get submerged. If you've previously mentioned the nearby volcano or the occasional underground tremors, readers will believe the eruption or the earthquake.

Also consider the plot and its themes. If the villain commits murders by throwing victims off the cliff, then the eroded cliff collapsing and taking the house into the depths will feel right. If barrels of gunpowder are stored in the underground chamber, an explosion is perfect. If the owners postponed the expense of having smoke detectors and sprinklers installed, then a flaming inferno is appropriate.

The house's neglected, part-decayed state may contribute to the collapse. Walls that were only superficially patched up after the previous earthquake will tumble easily, woodworm-damaged rafters will break, and neglected sprinkler systems will fail.

WHERE IS THE MC?

If possible, let the MC be present at the destruction, so the readers can experience this through her eyes and ears.

She may be standing outside in the garden, helplessly watching as the flames devour the building. She maybe a distance away and watch, mesmerised by the orange glow and columns of dark smoke that she knows signals the end of the Gloomy House. She could be inside – perhaps locked into the attic or the underground chamber, and struggles dramatically to escape and survive. She might even be the one who set fire to the place.

DESCRIBE THE DESTRUCTION IN DETAIL

The destruction is the dramatic highlight of the story. Indulge the reader in a great show.

Describe the colour of the flames and the columns of smoke rising against the night sky, the sound of shattering glass and splintering beams. Show how a wall quivers, sways and finally tumbles in slow motion.

Share details – how the flames climb up the brocade curtains of the dining room, how the roof timbers fall into the secret attic of the forbidden west wing, how the balcony (where bigamous John proposed to Mary) breaks off the facade.

For inspiration, watch videos of real disasters. You can find clips on sites like Vimeo and YouTube, showing practically any type of destruction, and you may be amazed at the vivid details you can glean from them.

Tip: If the Gloomy House in your story ends in a fire, make sure there's more smoke than flames. An exasperated firefighter told me that fiction writers and movie makers always use too much flame and not enough smoke. So, remember to add a generous quantity of smoke in many shades of grey.

Use plenty of sounds, the more, the better. Let the Dog howl. (Tip: Readers like it when the innocent animals escape.)

Use other senses – smell, temperature, pain, balance etc., whatever is relevant to the scenario.

WHERE'S THE VILLAIN?

The villain may perish in the house. Make this dramatic, so it doesn't feel like a Deus Ex Machina ploy. (In the ancient world, theatre plays often ended with a god emerging out of nowhere – with the help of a hidden machine – and miraculously solving everything in a convenient way.)

If possible, let it be his own choice in some way. Maybe he is safe in the garden, but decides to dash back into the house to rescue what matters to him most: the treasure chest (if he's the Greedy Villain), his invented apparatus (if he's the Obsessed Scientist) or the Helpless Child (if he has a conscience and a compassionate side).

WHEN DOES THIS HAPPEN?

In a novel, this is probably the climax scene, two thirds or three quarters into book. In a short story, it's often the final scene.

IS IT NECESSARY FOR THE HOUSE TO BE DESTROYED?

No. If it suits your story, the house can survive – for example, if your MC marries its owner, and they plan to renovate it and live there happily ever after.

You could still destroy part of the house – preferably the wing where the evil deeds took place.

EXAMPLES FROM LITERATURE

Rebecca, by Daphne du Maurier

The road to Manderley lay ahead. There was no moon. The sky above our heads was inky black. But the sky on the horizon was not dark at all. It was shot with crimson, like a splash of blood. And the ashes blew towards us with the salt wind from the sea.

The Gabriel Hounds, by Mary Stewart

The scene was like something from a coloured film of epic proportions. The walls towered black and jagged against the leaping flames behind them, and one high roof, burning fiercely, was now nothing but a crumbling grid of beams. Windows pulsed with light. With every gust of the breeze great clouds of pale smoke, filled with sparks, rolled down and burst over the crowd which besieged the main gate, and the Arabs scattered, shouting and cursing and laughing with excitement, only to bunch again nearer the gate as the cloud dispersed.

Touch Not the Cat, by Mary Stewart

It came in a tidal wave, that smashed through the ancient walls of the maze and broke, filthy, and swirling with the weight of the whole moat behind it, against the pavilion. The old structure seemed to shake and groan as if it would tear from its moorings in the grass, and buck away down the flood like a ship dragging her anchor. Then the water found its way in. There was a choking, fighting eternity, in which every second seemed like an hour, when the water pounded the gaping walls, spurting through with terrifying power. The jets shot in from every side, splashing and swirling together to join in a whirlpool which started, as rapidly as a sink filling under the taps, to rise from ankle to crouching thigh, to waist, to breasts...

PROFESSIONAL TIP

If you want to end the book on a bittersweet note rather than a full-on happily ever after, let one of the characters die in the disaster. Make this heart-wrenching yet satisfying by choosing one of the part-good part-evil characters. He sacrifices himself to save a helpless person who would otherwise have perished. This gives your story ending poignancy.

WHAT NOT TO DO

Don't rush this scene. This would deprive readers of the glorious drama and excitement.

ASSIGNMENTS

1. Decide how you will destroy the Gloomy House.

2. Do some research about this type of destruction, e.g. by watching videos.

3. Write three sentences describing sounds heard during the destruction. (Later, you'll insert them into different parts of the scene.)

4. Write three sentences describing slow-motion visuals of a detail of the destruction. (Later, you'll insert them into different parts of the scene.)

5. Write a (very rough) first draft of the scene.

CHAPTER 22

VISCERALS: STIR UP THE READER'S EMOTIONS

Gothic Fiction is very emotional. It aims to stir intense feelings in the reader. You can put your readers through a whole kaleidoscope of emotions – hope, fear, suspicion, euphoria, relief, terror, panic, foreboding, disgust, admiration, hatred, love, jealousy, or whatever suits your story – but the emotions must be intense. Your readers must be moved.

How do you achieve this?

One of my favourite techniques works supremely well in Gothic Fiction: the use of visceral reactions.

Let the reader feel what the PoV character feels. But don't spell out the emotion. Phrases like 'she was sad' or 'he felt remorse' won't affect the reader much.

Instead, describe the physical symptoms of that emotion. Where in the body does she feel it? How does it feel? Is the sensation hot or cold, pleasant or painful, expanding or tight? Does it itch, throb, churn or tingle?

Write a sentence about it. You can include the name of the emotion if you wish, although this is often not necessary.

If a fiction character is remorseful, a novice might write *'he felt remorse'* which is bland and leaves the reader untouched.

Now consider a remorseful person's visceral reactions: lump in the throat, runny nose, dull heavy feeling in the chest or all over the body, abdomen feels filled with knots, stomach feels weak or hard, nausea, loss of appetite, inability to sleep.

You might use these to write one of these sentences:

She tried to swallow the lump in her throat.

Her abdomen filled with knots.

A dull heaviness filled her chest.

She tossed in her bed, unable to sleep.

Remorse knotted her stomach.

Remorse clogged her throat.

She nibbled at the sweetmeat, unable to summon an appetite.

Let's take another emotion: desire. When a character desires someone or something, the physical symptoms include awareness of one's own heartbeat, warmth flooding the body, increased saliva in the mouth, tingling all over or just in the hands, fingers aching with the need to touch the person or object, faster breath, a pang in the heart area, a pleasant shiver all over or just in the upper body. (Erotic desire brings an additional set of reactions which I won't describe here.)

You might write sentences like these:

Her breath came faster, and her heart danced.

Warmth filled her chest, her heart, her mind.

Her fingers tingled.

Her palms burned with the need to touch his skin.

A pang in her chest released waves of yearning.

To find the right 'symptoms' of an emotion, draw on your own experience. How does desire feel to you? Where in the body have you felt anger?

QUICK THESAURUS FOR EMOTION VISCERALS

I've compiled some of the emotions that frequently come up in Gothic Fiction, and the typical visceral reactions the PoV character might experience. Feel free to use them, although I recommend that you describe them in creative ways in your own voice.

Anxiety, Nervousness

Thirst, tingling in the limbs, slight dizziness, churning in the stomach, contracting stomach, tightening chest, faster breathing, one's insides are 'quivering'.

Apprehension, Dread

The chest tingles, chills even when it's warm, cold fingers, goose-pimples on the skin, small hairs on the arms or at the nape of the neck rising, itching scalp, the heartbeat is heavy or sluggish, the stomach 'rolls', dizziness, shaking limbs, the bladder feels full (need to use the toilet), the throat feels tight and swallowing is difficult, the back of the throat hurts, sour taste in the mouth, a weight seems to press on the chest, wobbly knees, unpleasant cold tingle along the spine, a crawling sensation on the skin.

Desire

Breathing faster, awareness of one's own heartbeat, warmth flooding the body, increased saliva, tingling all over the body or just in the hands, fingers or palms aching with the need to touch the person or object, a pang in the heart area, a pleasant shiver either just in the upper body or all over.

Determination

Stronger and slightly faster heartbeat, a 'fluttering' sensation in the chest, muscles tightening.

Doubt, Suspicion

Heaviness in the abdomen, knotted stomach, quivering stomach, fast breath, thumping heartbeat, adrenaline rush.

Excitement

Fast pulse, breathlessness, heightened senses, adrenaline rush, lightness in the chest, dry mouth.

Fear, Terror

Chest so tight that it hurts, stomach feels hard like a lump of rock, shaky limbs, weak legs, trying to speak but no sound comes, racing heartbeat, heart thudding so violently it threatens to burst the chest, inability to move from the spot, hypersensitivity to sounds, dizziness, clenched jaw, not feeling pain from injuries, painful chest or throat, hyperventilating, bladder feels very full, urgent need to use the toilet, bladder opens.

Gratitude

Warmth all over the face and body, tingling limbs, relaxation, wide expanding chest.

Guilt

Tight chest, loss of appetite, stomach upset, thickness or pain in the throat.

Happiness, Elation

Warmth spreading throughout the body, the heart beats fast and loudly like a drum in the chest, a feeling of sunshine in one's head or chest, tingling hands, feeling alive, feeling rejuvenated, lightness in the limbs, urge to dance or skip, slight breathlessness.

Hope

A jolt through the body, tingling limbs, a 'fluttering' in the abdomen, lightheadedness, breath hitches, a sense of 'floating' above ground.

Love

Pulse races, the heart bangs strongly and loudly, weak knees or thighs, the tongue seems tangled in knots when one tries to speak, electrical tingling across the skin when accidentally touching the person, stomach feels hollow, fluttering in the abdomen, warmth spreads through the body when thinking of the person.

Remorse, Regret

Lump in the throat, runny nose, dull heavy feeling in the chest or all over the body, abdomen feels filled with knots, stomach feels weak or hard, nausea, loss of appetite, inability to sleep.

Sadness, Grief

Tears welling up especially when the person or topic is mentioned, blurred vision, crying, sobbing, hot eyelids, sore or scratchy throat, the chest aches, the heart hurts like it's breaking apart, the whole body feels cold, fatigue, heavy limbs, tight chest, the world seems to move much faster or much slower than usual.

Shock

Sudden coldness starting in the body's core and spreading, heaviness in the stomach, disorientation, dizziness, weak knees, nausea, cold sweats, racing heartbeat, seeing some things with utter clarity and others blurred.

Surprise

Tingling skin, fast heartbeat, breathlessness, fluttering in the abdomen, adrenaline rush, dizziness.

Worry

Dry mouth, tight throat, loss of appetite, sensitive stomach with digestive problems, a weight pressing down on one's chest and shoulders, headaches.

VARY THE EMOTIONAL INTENSITY

Feelings aren't static. They rise and subside, flare up and simmer. Make your scene more interesting and realistic by varying the intensity of the emotions.

A single visceral response or body language cue indicates a mild feeling. When the emotion gets intense, insert several visceral responses or body language cues close together.

Here are three variations of the same sentence showing Mary's fear, with one, two and three visceral responses. As you can see, the one with three is the most intense.

Mary's mouth went dry.

Mary's mouth went dry and her heart thumped.

Mary's mouth went dry, her heart thumped, and the hair lifted on the nape of her neck.

PROFESSIONAL TIP

If the PoV feels the same emotion throughout the scene, the effect on the reader wears off. Instead, use related emotions, perhaps starting with a mild version.

For example, in a scary scene, the PoV character feels apprehension at first, then fear. For a while, she experiences sheer terror. Then the danger passes, and the terror gives way to dread because she knows the monster will be back.

Apprehension, fear, terror and dread are closely related emotions – similar, but not the same.

WHAT NOT TO DO

Don't apply visceral reactions with a heavy brush – not even in an emotionally intense Gothic tale. If you overuse them with a symptom in every paragraph of your story, your writing will feel heavy and the readers may find it tedious.

Instead, cluster several visceral responses when you want to emphasise emotions, and keep other sections visceral-free.

FURTHER STUDY

For those of you who want to expand your emotion-writing skills, my book *Writing Vivid Emotions* shows a variety of techniques. It also contains a more comprehensive 'thesaurus' of visceral clues for emotions.

ASSIGNMENT

Choose three moments in your story where the PoV character feels a specific emotion. (Three different emotions.)

For each, write a sentence about one or two physical symptoms.

CHAPTER 23

MAKE IT CREAK AND CRACKLE: SOUNDS BUILD SUSPENSE

Of all the senses, the sense of hearing serves best to create suspense and excitement, and unlike other sensory descriptions, it doesn't slow the pace.

For every scene in your Gothic novel or story, think of noises the MC hears, and share them with the reader.

FOOTSTEPS

Whenever you want to create suspense, describe the sound of footsteps – the MC's own, or another character's. Depending on the person's gait and the type of footwear, steps may click, clack, clank, thump, thud, slap, whisper, shuffle.... The steps and floorboards underfoot may also make sounds, especially in old buildings where they may creak or groan.

Use the sound of footsteps to alert the MC to the villain's approach. This builds great suspense.

When the MC tries to move noiselessly so nobody guesses where she's going, describe the sound of her steps, and the reader will share her fear of discovery.

DOORS

Describe the noise of doors opening and closing. Especially in old derelict buildings with unoiled hinges, these can be creepy sounds which serve to build a spooky atmosphere and ratchet up the suspense. Depending on the type of door, it may creak, squeal, screech, grate, whine, hiss, buzz, hum, groan, clank, thud.... Pressing the door handle, turning the knob or twisting the key will also create noises.

For ideas how to apply the 'door' effects, see the chapter 'The Door of the Doomed: Heightening Suspense'.

WEATHER

The weather creates its own noises. Rain may tap, hammer or slosh against windowpanes and gurgle down drainpipes. Thunder may roil, rip, roll, crash or boom. Wind (and storm) can whisper or rustle in the leaves, creak the branches, rattle the shutters, howl around corners, whine in the chimney, slap against the facade. When the wind is still, the MC is likely to hear animals: birds, crickets, bees.

THE BUILDING

Water gurgles down a drainpipe. Cutlery rattles, crockery clonks, a tea kettle hisses, curtains swish, and a ceiling fan whirrs. In old derelict buildings, there may be roof timbers creaking for no apparent reason, and of course there could be rodent feet scurrying above the MC's head in the attic.

PROFESSIONAL TIP

Whenever the MC is forced to stay inactive while waiting for something crucial to happen, whether she fears or desires it, insert a sentence describing a sound. This turns up the tension several notches.

Here's an example:

"I warned you to stay away from the laboratory. Now you've found out. I cannot let you live."

The knife came closer to her throat. And closer.

She tried to scream through the gag and strained against the fetters, knowing it to be useless.

Gears clanked. Liquids bubbled and hissed. Somewhere in the wall, water gurgled down a drainpipe.

The cold edge of steel touched her skin. She tried not to swallow.

EXAMPLES FROM LITERATURE

The Gabriel Hounds, by Mary Stewart

...a rusty nail fell from its socket with a clink that made me jump, and the rustle of plaster falling after it sounded like a puff of wind in dry leaves.

Nine Coaches Waiting, by Mary Stewart

The ghastly minutes crawled by. The night was still, held in its pall of mist. I could hear the occasional soft drip of moisture from the boughs that hung over us, and once some stray current of air must have stirred the trees, for the budded twigs pawed at the roof. Below in the boathouse the hollow slap and suck of water told of darkness and emptiness and a world of nothing.

Wuthering Heights, by Emily Bronte

There was no sound but the moaning wind, which shook the windows every now and then, the faint crackling of the coals, and the click of my snuffers as I removed at intervals the long wick of the candle.

WHAT NOT TO DO

Don't ignore sound effects as a tool for creating atmosphere, suspense and excitement.

FURTHER STUDY

If you want to learn how to keep your readers terrified, my book *Writing Scary Scenes* will teach you many useful techniques.

ASSIGNMENTS

1. Visualise the scene you're currently writing or plan to write next. Imagine the noises the MC might hear, and compile a list of at least ten. Try to find vivid verbs to describe the sounds. (Not just "There were footsteps on the stairs" but "footsteps clanked down the stairs."

2. Next time the weather is windy where you live, listen to its noises, whether out of doors or inside. Describe them.

CHAPTER 24

MUST AND DUST: DETAILS OF DECAY

The Gloomy House is probably in a dilapidated state, neglected either through lack of funds or lack of care. Perhaps it is so big that the owner's family inhabit only one wing and leave the rest to the bats and rats.

The residents may no longer even notice the tell-tale signs of decay – but the newly arrived MC will. Here are some ideas you can incorporate, depending on how dilapidated you want the place to be:

- creaking floorboards

- expensive carpets in the main reception rooms, elsewhere cheap low-quality carpets or bare concrete

- expensive, once-valuable carpets... but they're threadbare and/or stained

- the ceiling is stained with the traces of old water leaks, and during heavy rain the water may drip down

- cobwebs in the ceiling corners of the rooms

- dead insects on windowsills

- a thick layer of dust on the sideboards and other surfaces

- under the bed, a thick layer of dust with dead insects

- light switches are grimy and feel sticky to the touch

- windowpanes are so grimy, dusty and full of cobwebs that they let in only little light

- big cracks in the window pains, and perhaps sections of the glass are missing

- doors don't shut properly

- doors and shutters rattle in the wind

- chipped and cracked tableware

- unoiled creaking hinges on cupboards

- furniture drawers are stuck

- stained mattresses

- table surface is stained with rings from glasses and cups

- black soot on wall and ceiling around the woodstove

- potted houseplants are dried up, yellow, dead or dying

- creepy-crawlies scuttle across the floor (research the type prevalent in that part of the world, e.g. cockroaches or millipedes)

- a smell of old urine

- curtains are faded, with sections of the once richly-coloured fabric gone pale

- moth holes in textiles

- junk in drawers, e.g. dried-up cosmetics, medicine bottles years past their use-by date

- the heating or air-conditioning system isn't working

EXAMPLES FROM LITERATURE

These three excerpts are from different sections of *The Gabriel Hounds* by Mary Stewart:

The walls, high and blind, showed here and there the remains of some coloured decoration, ghostly patterns and mosaics and broken marble plastered over and painted a pale ochre colour which had baked white with the strong sunlight.

At the foot of each pillar stood a carved marble trough for flowering plants. These were still full of soil, but now held only grass and some tightly clenched, greyish-looking buds. There was one spindly tamarisk hanging over the broken coping of the pool. Somewhere, a cicada purred gently. Grey thistles grew in the gaps of the pavement, and the pool was dry.

Set right back in the corner of the upper room or dais was a huge bed, which at one time must have been a luxurious affair with legs shaped like dragon's claws, a high carved headboard, and hanging from the ceiling above it some sort of gilt device resembling a bird, which was supposed to have held bed-drapes in its talons. Now one wing of the bird was broken, the gilt was flaked and dirty, and from the claws hung only a couple of rubbed velvet curtains which could have been any shade from dark red to black, and which sagged in big loops down on either side of the bed-head, almost concealing with their heavy swags of shadow the figure which reclined in a welter of rugs and blankets.

HOW DO THE OWNERS FEEL ABOUT THE DECAY?

Decide what the owner's attitude is. Is he embarrassed that he cannot afford repairs? Does he pretend that he's wealthy, and seek to cover up the problems, e.g. by hiding the mould on the walls with tapestries? Or perhaps he's oblivious to the decay, so used to the place that he no longer notices the problems. Another possibility is that he is stingy and will hoard the money instead of spending it on much-needed repairs, or maybe he puts every cent into his scientific researches.

You need to know what his attitude is, so he will react accordingly when visitors discover the state of decay.

PROFESSIONAL TIP

Don't just rely on visual descriptions to show the decay, but use several senses (especially sound, smell and touch). Let the MC discover the neglected state through action. For example, she may stumble across a loose floorboard or be unable to push the jammed drawer back into the cupboard. Maybe she volunteers to cook dinner, and finds cockroaches and silverfish in the food jars. Or perhaps she tries to pull the curtains, and the pull comes off in her hand.

WHAT NOT TO DO

Don't dump the whole description at the beginning. Instead, sprinkle small bits throughout the scene.

FURTHER STUDIES

If you enjoy setting descriptions and want to make the most of them, consult my book *Writing Vivid Settings* which contains many advanced techniques.

ASSIGNMENT

Choose one room in the Gloomy House. This can be any room you choose – the attic, the staircase, the dining room, or wherever a scene of your story plays out. Make a list of five to ten signs of decay an observer can notice in this room.

CHAPTER 25

CRIMSON AS IF SOAKED IN BLOOD: THE COLOUR RED

Red, more than any other colour, evokes emotions – and it magnifies emotions that have already been awakened in the reader. This works on a subconscious level. The reader won't be aware of what you're doing.

By using the colour red, you can evoke passion, danger, warning, love, prohibition, lust, heat, aggression, dominance, sin, debt, power, hurt... and all those are perfect emotions for Gothic stories.

Find something you can make red: perhaps the master of the Gloomy House wants his new bride to wear a dress of red velvet.... Maybe the man in the antique painting wears a red waistcoat.... The stair rug on the sweeping staircase could be red... or the curtains in the gloomy dining room are.... The painter may pick up red from his palette.... The jewels that get stolen are precious rubies....

Any shade of red works well, but rich and intense nuances are best: crimson, vermilion, carmine, scarlet, burgundy, purple.

You can state the colour outright ('a dress of crimson velvet') or describe it, for example by comparing it to something else. If comparing, use creative language hinting at wealth, decadence, power, decay or violence. For example, the colour of a dress might be the 'rich colour of rubies', 'the colour of a cardinal's cloak', 'the colour of spilled wine' or 'the colour of crushed strawberries'.

OTHER GOTHIC COLOURS

While red is the most effective colour, you can also achieve great Gothic effects with the colours black and white.

Black evokes secrets and dark deeds, while white suggests innocence, naivete and victimhood.

This doesn't mean that the villain needs to wear black and the victim white... you can mix things up. The innocent bride may wear a black dress while the villain is dressed in red, and the tablecloth is white as baking flour.

There mere mention of those colours – especially if creatively described – intensifies the emotional impact of a scene. You don't need to apply them as direct symbols.

EXAMPLES FROM LITERATURE

In most Gothic classics, this technique is applied so subtly that the reader will not consciously notice it – although now you're aware, you'll easily spot it in the next Gothic novel you read.

Here are two examples of overt use: In *Jane Eyre* by Charlotte Bronte, the child Jane gets locked into the 'red room' which terrifies her. In *Sunshine* by Robin McKinley, the villain forces the MC to wear a revealing red dress, to make her an attractive victim for a hungry vampire.

PROFESSIONAL TIP

Apply the red colour to an object you want to draw attention to.

WHAT NOT TO DO

Don't rely on this technique alone to create reader emotion. It works best if combined with other techniques.

ASSIGNMENT

Think of an object in your story that's red. Curtains, cushions, a carpet, a garment, a jewel....

Describe in a few words. This can be a partial sentence, a full sentence or (if the item plays a role in the plot) a whole paragraph.

CHAPTER 26

HOW TO CONVEY YOUR NOVEL'S MESSAGE WITHOUT PREACHING

Reading a novel can help readers grow wiser, because they learn from the MC's dilemmas and mistakes. They gain life lessons without having to undergo the tough trial themselves. A novel can also alert readers to environmental or social problems by providing information they would otherwise ignore.

Gothic Fiction, more than most other genres, arouses readers' emotions in a way that makes the mind receptive to moral and ethical messages. So if you want to raise awareness for a cause, you can use your Gothic novel as a vehicle.

In early (18th century) Gothic Fiction, the message was usually simple: "Good triumphs over evil." That's a bit too pat to satisfy most modern readers.

In the 19th century, authors used Gothic novels to draw attention to social issues often relating to gender or class. By highlighting fictional characters' plights, they could expose the abuse of power, and the injustice of the law. When you read 19th century novels through the lens of social criticism, you may be astonished how passionate and outspoken those authors were about issues close to their heart. The message 'Good triumphs over evil' was still there. It was more or less obligatory in the 19th century. But now the authors highlighted the plight of governesses, the vulnerability of women due to legal inequality, the need for a divorce law to provide a way out of desperately unhappy marriages, and other issues – including problems that Victorians would not even dare talk about.

Not all short stories carry a message – but without one, they're quickly forgotten. In a novel, there may be more than one message.

The message can dominate the story, or be applied with such a light brush that the reader is barely aware of it while reading. Either is fine.

Some writers set out to create a novel that highlights a specific issue they feel strongly about – whether that's human trafficking, abortion, animal abuse, the pollution of rivers or the unfair working conditions of inner-city schoolteachers. Others write a complete draft first, and only then consider what the message might be. They expand and strengthen this message during the rewriting.

You can choose any message you like. Even just highlighting a social issue so the readers become more aware of it is a valid message.

With Gothic Fiction, the most natural fit is the helplessness of a certain population segment against injustice or abuse. Choose a population segment that's vulnerable, and that's involved in your plot somehow (perhaps as the MC, perhaps as the villain's victim).

You may choose the elderly, the mentally ill, refugees, prison parolees, recovering alcoholics, impressionable teenagers, orphans, domestic workers, illegal immigrants, debtors, the poor, gypsies, the homeless, the unemployed… whoever you feel are vulnerable to injustice and abuse in some way and would need more protection.

You don't need to choose a population group that everyone thinks of as helpless. If you can show that theatre actors, plumbers or orthodontic dentists are especially vulnerable to injustice or abuse in certain situations, the readers will certainly learn from this, and the story will have impact. But for this to work, you need to understand the vulnerabilities of actors, schoolteachers or doctors so you can write about their plight with plausibility.

Flagging up the helplessness of a social group is a natural fit for Gothic Fiction, but it's not the only option. If you want to convey a different message – perhaps you want to call for religious tolerance, encourage people to be more generous, advise truthfulness in all circumstances, or promote forgiveness – then by all means, use your story to illustrate that message.

EXAMPLES FROM LITERATURE

Wuthering Heights (the original novel by Emily Bronte, not the cute-ified movie versions) speaks to us about raw hatred, passionate revenge and the healing power of forgiveness.

Victorian author Wilkie Collins had studied law, and he used his fiction to draw attention to unfair laws, especially the legal inequality of women, the discrimination against children of unmarried parents, and healthy but unwanted people sent to lunatic asylums by their relatives. You may want to read his most famous novel *The Woman in White* in this light.

WHAT NOT TO DO

Avoid 'preachy' writing. Modern readers rarely tolerate novels with a heavy-handed moral message. Instead, apply the message with such a light brush that the reader is barely aware of it while reading the story, and only starts to think about it afterwards.

ASSIGNMENT:

1. Do you have a message you want to get across in your story? (If you have only a vague idea, write it down anyway. As long as you're aware of it, it will crystallise later. You can refine it once you've penned the first draft of your tale.)

2. What social group is shown in your story as vulnerable (to abuse or injustice)? Could their plight be the message to the readers?

CHAPTER 27

MIX AND MATCH: LAYERING GENRES

Gothic Fiction blends beautifully with other genres. You can use the techniques learned in this guide to enrich whatever genre you normally write, to intensify a work-in-progress, or to power up the draft of a novel that's not exciting enough.

Here are some ideas on how to combine Gothic with other genres.

GOTHIC ROMANCE

Gothic and Romance are a natural pairing, because both are emotionally intense and passion filled.

Put the love story at the centre of your novel – but to differ from traditional Romance, don't reveal immediately who the MC's true love is. Present several attractive candidates, and keep the reader guessing until the middle of the novel, perhaps even until the Climax. The Love Interest may turn out to be the Semi-Outsider, the Ally Outside, the True Heir... or even a formerly villainous character who has repented and reformed. If your story is Gothic Paranormal Romance, he could even be a vampire, werewolf or other fantasy creature. The other suitors may be revealed as the Evil Charmer, the Abusive Guardian, the Greedy Villain.

Although Gothic Romance readers enjoy being kept in suspense about who the true love is, the novel's ending must make the answer clear. Readers want to be confident that this couple are meant to be together, that they have solved their problems, that he is truly a reformed character who will not stray from the path of virtue again, and that they are able to deal with future challenges together.

Perhaps the love is initially forbidden – because one of the couple is still married (or believes himself married), because they assume they're half-siblings, or because some other taboo prevents their union. However, it's best to introduce the forbidden love as a story complication, not the sole basis for the plot.

Create romantic, atmospheric descriptions. Show beauty and romance even when describing the decay. Include sensory descriptions, involving especially the sense of touch. Avoid gross, graphic and revolting descriptions. Be careful especially when evoking the sense of smell. Don't disgust the reader with nauseating odours. A musky smell in an unused room is the maximum Romance readers are willing to stomach.

Focus on positive emotions – love, compassion, yearning, desire, hope – and keep the negative ones limited to what the plot requires. Of course the MC can feel disappointment, jealousy, grief and fear – but avoid revulsion and disgust.

GOTHIC HORROR

Horror is another emotionally intense form of fiction, and often layered with Gothic elements.

The focus is on suspense, and the Gloomy House is the central location where terrible things happen. The story can feature paranormal or fantasy elements, or it can revolve around human evil.

Use the full palette of the fear emotions – apprehension, dread, horror, terror, panic, etc. Play up the creepiness and suspense. Employ sensory descriptions, especially sounds, and don't shy away from graphic descriptions if the plot requires them.

Darkness and semi-darkness are effective for scaring readers, so you may want to set some scenes in the evening, at night or in a windowless cellar. Perhaps twilight gives way to night, maybe a seance or a haunting takes place after the clock strikes twelve, the

Obsessed Scientist carries out experiments in absolute darkness, or the MC is held captive in a dungeon where no daylight penetrates.

GOTHIC HISTORICAL

At the time the story plays out, the Gloomy House is already old and dilapidated, so research the architecture and furnishing styles of an earlier period.

What social conflicts were prevalent in that era? Was it a time of class or gender struggles, of slavery or abolition? Perhaps colonialisation, military conquest, war, child labour, unemployment, famine or forced emigration were features of daily life for many people then. Weave one or more of these issues into your plot.

Bigamy is a great plot element for periods when divorce was not an option. Which character is already married – but hides the fact in order to marry someone else, or is unaware that his spouse is still alive? Perhaps the bigamy took place in a previous generation, rendering a presumed marriage invalid, and when discovered, changes the family inheritance.

Be aware of how moral standards differed. For example, a 19th century man might go to great lengths to hide his homosexuality, because he fears being sentenced to prison. This will allow you to add period-authentic and believable conflicts and secrets to the plot.

GOTHIC SCIENCE FICTION

Science or technology plays a big part in this genre mash-up, either in the background or as a core plot element.

When envisaging the future world, look at the technological developments of two different future periods: the one when the Gloomy House was equipped, and the later one, when the story unfolds. At the time of the novel's events, the once state-of-the art technology of the Gloomy House is already out of date.

When writing Hard Science Fiction, the story probably revolves around or derives from a scientific discovery or technological invention. What is this invention? What guilty secret made it possible?

If your story is Social Science Fiction, focus on a prevalent conflict of that time. Is it a conflict of class, gender, culture, ethnicity or what? How does this conflict play out in the Gloomy House? Which residents of the Gloomy House are on which side in this conflict, and what are the individual attitudes? How aware is the MC of this conflict when she arrives, and what does she learn during her stay?

GOTHIC STEAMPUNK

When layering Steampunk and Gothic Fiction, use your imagination to equip the Gloomy House with steampunk technology, e.g. devices powered by clockwork mechanisms, gas and steam. Think especially of the noises created by these appliances – the ticking, clicking and rattling, the hissing and squealing – because those can serve as suspense-increasing background sounds.

The Obsessed Scientist character and his work may feature greatly in Gothic Steampunk stories.

Make the most of the novel's Climax, the destruction of the Gloomy House. The MC should be present, inside the house and in great danger.

GOTHIC FANTASY

The crime has probably been committed years – or generations – ago, perhaps because of a forbidden passion such as incest or bigamy. The repercussions affect the living: there may be a curse on the family, a guilty ghost haunts the castle, or clans are engaged in an endless blood feud.

The Gloomy House is probably a castle and the underground chamber is a dungeon. Alternatively, it could be the cottage where an eccentric magician lives as a hermit, or a network of caves leading deep into the bowels of the earth.

The residents of the Gloomy House may include paranormal or mythological creatures, e.g. vampires or dragons. A werewolf may fulfil the role of the Dog character.

GOTHIC THRILLER

Gothic thrillers are suspenseful and creepy and build up to a scary crescendo.

The Gloomy House probably serves two purposes. Officially, it's a hotel, retirement home, children's holiday camp, nature observation station or artist colony – but this is merely the front for nefarious activities. What really goes on is sheer evil. Think of a serious, large-scale organised crime the readers will care about: organ harvesting from unwilling donors, child trafficking, white slavery, drug smuggling, manufacturing biological weapons of mass destruction, deliberate environmental pollution, production of snuff films....

The centre of the terrible deeds is the underground chamber, and during the novel's terrifying Black Moment, the MC herself becomes the victim and is held captive there. She probably escapes during the Climax, when the Gloomy House gets destroyed. She may even bring about the destruction herself, at the risk of her own life.

The novel has several villains, and the MC (and the reader) discovers them one by one. One of these villains is a person the MC had liked and trusted. Make the most of the trust, suspicion and betrayal issues. (More about that in the chapter 'Trust No One: Suspicion, Resentment and Betrayal'.)

GOTHIC COSY MYSTERY

A murder has been committed – and inheritance is the motive (although it could be a red herring). An eccentric last will and valuable old jewels probably play a role. The body, or an important clue, may be found among the dusty bookshelves in the library.

Give every character a guilty secret to hide, which, when discovered, makes them suspects.

At the end of the novel, when all the characters are assembled in the library (or dining room, or other place in the Gloomy House), the sleuth reveals their secrets one by one.

The Gothic Cosy Mystery has more suspense and passion than the 'normal' Cosy Mystery. However, avoid shocking and terrifying your readers.

MIDDLE GRADE (Children's fiction)

The MC is a child who gets sent to spend her holidays (American English: vacations) in a place where she's never been (the Gloomy House) with people she doesn't know. Make the story exciting and even frightening, but avoid graphic violence, eroticism and perversions.

The Dog character may play a major role.

YA (Young Adult aka Teenage Fiction)

The MC is alone in the world, perhaps because she's newly orphaned, or because her uncaring guardians have dumped the responsibility for her on someone else. Maybe she gets sent to live with a distant relative, or maybe strangers are paid to take her in. Another possibility is that she has fled an abusive home and needs a place that will provide bed and board until she can sort out a longer-term solution. Either way, she soon discovers that she is not wanted.

Although eroticism, perversions and violence can play a role in YA fiction, don't indulge in them.

However, you can make parts of the story seriously scary.

Let the MC grow through her ordeal. Perhaps someone tries to use her for his evil deeds, and at first she falls for his ploy (and maybe for him), but then she discovers the truth and refuses to cooperate any longer. During this experience, she develops ethical values, gains integrity, and becomes strong.

HUMOUR

Horror and humour always go well together, and Gothic tropes lend themselves to satire. Re-read chapter 'The Tropes of Gothic Fiction', pile on the tropes and exaggerate them.

When using the characters, feel free to combine them in surprising or even ridiculous ways, i.e. the Obsessed Scientist is also the Ghost, the Dog is the Greedy Villain, and the Corrupt Priest is the Bigamist.

EXAMPLES FROM LITERATURE

One you've learnt to recognise Gothic features, you'll easily spot the Gothic books in your favourite genre.

The Shining by Stephen King is Gothic Horror.

The Toll Gate by Georgette Heyer is Gothic Regency Romance.

The Hound of the Baskervilles by Sir Arthur Conan Doyle is Gothic Mystery.

Nocturne for a Widow by Amanda DeWees is Gothic Historical Mystery Romance (typical of the 21st century trend to mash up several genres)

PROFESSIONAL TIP

Novels layering several genres have greater sales potential than those with a single genre.

This was not always the case. In the 20th century, publishers and booksellers preferred books that could be put into a single specific genre shelf. In those days, multi-genre books stood little chance.

Now the opposite is true. Modern distribution methods allow placing a book on several genre shelves simultaneously, which means it gets seen by fans of different genres, and thus can reach much bigger audiences.

Use this trend to your advantage. Layer your main genre with Gothic Fiction (and perhaps with other genres) to extend the book's reach.

Fiction that touches on more than one category is called 'cross-genre'.

ASSIGNMENTS

1. What's your favourite genre to read? Think of novels you've read in this genre which have strong Gothic elements. Try to identify several, and reread them.

2. What genre do you normally write? If you haven't written much yet, which genre do you enjoy reading most? Brainstorm how to layer this genre with Gothic elements.

You can draw on the ideas I've listed above. Although I've given only a few examples, you can combine Gothic with any fiction genre. Use your creativity and layer away.

CHAPTER 28

A SAMPLE GOTHIC STORY: THE TRAIN TO DOLNO OREHOVO

Would you like to read one of my Gothic stories? This tale is set in Bulgaria (Eastern Europe) where I live.

The idea started to form on a hot day in August when I got off the train at Gorna Mahala instead of Dolna Mahala. For hours, I sat outside the dilapidated station house, feeding the hungry stray cats with pieces of banitsa and wondering when another train would come. Exhausted from the day's sightseeing and the heat, I closed my eyes and pursued every fiction writer's favourite question: "What if…?"

I developed it in the style of Victorian ghost stories, with a slow pace, mounting suspense and creepy descriptions. A train fills the role of the Gloomy House, although there is also the dilapidated station building.

As you read my story, have fun spotting the Gothic tropes and plot elements discussed in this book.

THE TRAIN TO DOLNO OREHOVO

Rayne Hall

My thighs ache from hours of walking on steep village streets in the Rhodope Mountains, and my hot feet complain about being enclosed in sturdy shoes. I long to get back to the hotel, put my legs up on cool sheets and book a pedicure.

But first, I'll have to get a train to Gorno Orehovo or whatever that nest is called, then take a bus from there, then another train, a taxi.... At least, the walking part is over for today! For the rest of my holiday in Bulgaria, I'll stay by the pool, wear soft slippers and pamper my feet.

To my relief, the station's ticket counter is open for service. I use the sentence I've memorised from the Bulgarian Tourist Phrase Book."Ednoposochen billet do Gorno Orehovo, molya." *A one-way ticket to Gorno Orehovo, please.*

The woman behind the glass panel demands something in Bulgarian I don't understand.

I shrug my helplessness. "Ne raspiram. Az sum avstraliika." *I don't understand. I'm Australian.* I've said that a lot these past few days. For me as a language teacher, it's a matter of pride to have mastered some phrases of the local lingo.

A smile flits across her face. She places the change coins on the ledge before her and writes the price on a piece of paper for me to read: 8.80 leva.

I slide a 10 leva note through the slit under her window. A thin paper ticket whirs from the printer, and she circles the time on it. Oh, good, that's in just ten minutes! I won't have to wait for hours in the dry afternoon heat.

The clerk makes sure I understand that I have to disembark at the thirteenth stop: "Edno, dve, tri, chetiri..... trinaiset: Gorno Orehovo." While pushing the ticket through the window slit towards me, her other hand swipes the change coins into her lap.

Corruption in miniature.... Yet, one lev twenty stotinki – that's barely an Australian dollar. Many wages in Bulgaria are scarcely enough for survival, and this woman may desperately need a little extra money to feed her family. I wish I could tell her she's welcome to the tip, that she's earned it with her helpfulness. But my language skills aren't up to that, so I just smile and say, "Merci." *Thanks.* I rejoice at the loan word from French.

Outside, all the benches are occupied, so I study the obligatory statue on the forecourt – yet another revolutionary hero from the 1870s in socialist-realism concrete. Normally I like sculptures, but the charm of this particular style is wearing off.

The rails sing, and the train arrives. I hurry to climb into one of the brightly-graffitied carriages.

To my frustration, nobody moves their luggage off the seats to make room for me. I'll have to stand. Ah well, it's only a few stops until Gorno Orehovo, and from there I'll take a – hopefully comfortable – bus.

I lean against the wall to take the pressure off my aching legs. The air-conditioning isn't working. I'm not surprised, considering how hopelessly out of date and underfunded the Bulgarian railway network is.

The landscape passes: orchards alternating with yellow fields and pasture with flocks of goats, and increasingly steep slopes covered in dark pines. I count the stops to thirteen. Ah, here comes Gorno Orehovo. I proudly decipher the capital letters of the Cyrillic alphabet I've learned for this holiday: Горно Орехово.

The station is small and dilapidated, built many years ago in a blend of National Revival styleand Socialist Constructivism. Picturesque oriels jut out from a facade of grey concrete. The glass panels are shattered, the concrete tiles cracked, and the orange paint is peeling off the wood.

I stride into the shade of the waiting room to buy a bus ticket. Alas, the ticket counters are deserted, and debris piled along the wall. This station hasn't been staffed for a decade or more.

I look for the bus stop on the other side of the station. But there's no sign saying 'spirka' or 'avtobus', no timetable, not even an asphalted area where a bus might wait.

A stony track leads up the slope. Broad ruts show it's occasionally used by cars or carts, which suggests that it connects the train station with the village. The bus probably stops up there. I really hadn't meant to walk any more today, but it can't be helped. I force my aching legs onwards and upwards.

The air has the straw-smell of a hot summer's day. Grasses nod their long furred heads in the faint breeze. *Krekri, krekri* a bird screeches continuously.

Trudging uphill, I reach the settlement. Among cracked walls of ochre clay, chickens cackle and chained dogs bark.

An old man sits on a roadside bench, tapping his stick rhythmically on the ground. When I approach him with a courteous "dober den" he bares his teeth like an angry dog and taps his stick harder.

I drag myself onwards. Most houses are deserted, their roof beams collapsed, their walls half-eroded and their windows gaping in empty darkness. It's one of the many villages in Bulgaria where the population dwindles by a tenth every year, and only a few old people remain. Small wonder the railway company doesn't bother to maintain the station.

I spot an old woman on another bench and hurry towards her. She's wearing a dress made from the standard blue cloth issued during Bulgaria's communist era. Before I have time to utter a polite greeting, she raises her stick to block my way. "Kade?" *Where to?* she demands, in the tone of a border guard interrogating an illegal immigrant.

"Avtobusna spirka?" I think that's Bulgarian for *bus stop.*

She lets out a bark so unfriendly that I take a step back.

With her facial furrows and cold eyes, she reminds me of the evil witch in my childhood fairy tale book. She points her stick at me like a rapier, and issues more barked language.

I take another step backwards and say my sentence about being Australian, not understanding.

She repeats the same words, but in loud shouts. In response, the dogs in the neighbourhood bark in unison. The air vibrates with the sound of their anger.

I know when I'm not welcome, and I'm ready to retreat. I just need to know where to find the bus. "Molya, kade avtobus? Molya?" I beseech. *Please, where's the bus? Please?*

Her rapier-stick points westwards. "Dolno Orehovo."

She taps it on the ground. "Gorno Orehovo."

What... is she saying...? Realisation plunges like a lump down my gullet: I'm in the wrong village.

Two settlements have similar names, and I bought the ticket to the wrong one. There is no bus from here.

"Merci." I want to ask her how to get to Dolno Orehovo, the place where the buses leave, but she glowers so ferociously that I hurry away before I get skewered by her angry stick.

I walk back downslope to the station. My legs are aching seriously now. As a schoolteacher in Melbourne, I don't get much exercise.

The old witch pointed to the west, so Dolno Orehovo lies in that direction, and probably not far away. I flick on my smartphone as I walk and check the navigation app. The Orehovo nests don't warrant photos or street views, but at least they're just eight kilometres apart. Dolno Orehovo is the next stop on the railway line, so I'll take the first train there.

I return to the station's shade. There is no bench, neither on the platform nor in the waiting room. I guess they've all been appropriated by the villagers, and the blue witch was sitting on one of them.

In the absence of a bench, I sit on the steps leading from the station building to the platform, and slip off my shoes and socks. The concrete slabs are cracked and littered with white cigarette stubs.

The air is hot and still, and while there's a roof overhanging the square grey columns, the shade offers no respite from the heat.

I take a gulp of water. This morning, when I filled the bottle at a natural mineral spring, the water tasted cool and fresh. Now it's sun-warmed, flavourless and mildly disgusting. I pour it over my hot, swollen feet. They respond with gratitude and instantly feel better.

When will the next train come? If this station had a timetable, it's long gone, replaced by death notices. Bulgarians paste black-framed posters of their dearly departed, complete with photo and mini-biography, on every available surface: house walls, lamp posts, bus shelters, and, it seems, the cracked glass of abandoned railway stations.

I learn that Ivana Giorgeva Todorova and Todor Ivanov Giorgev have left this world, but can't deduce when this happened since parts of the posters have long been ripped away.

This station's obligatory public art is a concrete bas-relief on the facade, depicting scimitar-wielding Turkish oppressors slaughtering Bulgarian peasants. Bulgarians still bear a grudge against the Turks for five hundred years of occupation, and their national pride is based on the Liberation War. Gruesome atrocities happened in that final period, with whole villages put to the slaughter under Turkish scimitars. Practically every road, school and hospital is named after a hero from that era, while monuments and murals everywhere keep the memory of those massacres alive.

I've seen so many of those reliefs over the past days that I no longer even bother to get my camera out. I have more than enough illustrations for my blog post about socialist-realism art.

Two cats – a black and a tabby – stare at me with hungry eyes, but daren't approach. They're so skinny that the ribs stick out. I fish in my bag for the banitsa, a traditional Bulgarian pastry filled with cheese, break off some pieces and toss them towards the cats. They devour the offering greedily, fight for the last morsel, and beseech me for more.

The rails vibrate with a ringing tone, and a loud rumble announces an approaching train. I grab my shoes and jump up, ready to board. But it's a freight train that whooshes past.

What if there are no more trains today? What if the one I arrived in was the only passenger train still stopping in this god-forsaken place?

My throat tightens at the thought.

I rationalise. The train was scheduled, so it'll stop here again tomorrow. I'll be stranded for 24 hours at the most. I may be uncomfortable in the heat, but I'm in no danger. And I won't starve: I still have half a banitsa.

Maybe I shouldn't have wasted my last water on bathing my feet. At the thought of thirst, my throat yearns for liquid. My whole body suddenly feels parched. Can I survive a whole day without water? I tell myself that of course I can.

The cats come closer, begging, suffering and desperation driving them to the perceived danger. I give them the rest of my banitsa. However many hours pass before the next train, I'll eat again before long. The cats' need is greater than mine.

Along the track, straw-coloured plants stand in desiccated defiance. Green-black wooded slopes rise into a distant haze. The sky is a light pale blue, yellowing towards the horizon, featureless apart from a few feeble cumulus clouds. At least, the worst of the afternoon heat is receding as evening comes.

Will I have to spend the night in this forsaken place?

I can survive one night, I remind myself. Even if there's only one train a day, that train is bound to come without fail.

Unless for some reason, tomorrow's trains follow a different schedule. Like, if it's a Sunday.

My stomach clumps. Today is Saturday.

Cold sweat beads on my dry skin. I dare not think about being stuck here for two days.

Should I try to get back to the village, beg the witch to give me at least some water? But while I'm there, a train may stop and I can't afford to miss it.

Suddenly dizzy in the heat, I feel my head spinning.

Can I walk to Dolno Orehovo? It's the next station. Step by step, between the rails, railroad tie to railroad tie, I should be able to get there. But eight kilometres uphill on swollen, blistered feet is unthinkable.

Soon it will be night. I dread the thought of walking in the dark.

Already, the golden afternoon light dims. A greenish-grey haze spreads like a cooling mist, not what I'd expect at the end of a hot parching day.

I try to compose the blog post in my head. Rebels and gory massacres will appeal to my fifteen-year old students. But I'm too thirsty and tired to concentrate.

The rails sing. Hastily, I slip into my shoes and lace them. There's no time to bother with socks, in case it's a passenger train approaching.

Chuff-chuff, chuff-chuff, chuff-chuff pants the train over the rumble of wheels.

A black locomotive appears out of the mist. I know the Bulgarian railway system is seriously out of date, but I didn't know they still used steam trains. I wish I had time to get out the camera and take photos for my blog, but what matters right now is to board this train that will take me Dolno Orehovo.

I grab the nearest handrail, and climb up the steep steps at the end of a carriage. The door gives a brief squeal when I push it open.

The air inside the carriage is noticeably cooler than on the platform. However ancient the train, at least the air conditioning works. But the air is fetid, like the carriage hasn't been aired for months, with layered odours of sweat and decay.

Since I won't be travelling far, I choose a seat near the door, opposite three women in traditional crimson costume.

"Dober den," I greet, then correct myself, "Dober vecher." *Good day. Good evening.*

None of them returns my greeting.

I drop my backpack and sit down anyway. The wood-slatted bench is hard without any kind of upholstery.

It's really chilly here on this train. The skin on my arms pimples, and a cold trickle runs down my spine. This can't be air-conditioning, not on a train this old.

The women opposite me wear beautiful costumes with long crimson skirts, white blouses and black flower-embroidered aprons. The intense crimson of their headscarves emphasises the pallor of their faces. From the likeness of their features, I guess they're related, perhaps three generations of the same family. The youngest has nodded off, her head leaning against the window. The stout middle one is intent on crocheting some lace, while the grandmother clutches a flower-filled basket in gnarled hands and stares right past me as if I didn't exist.

"Dolno Orehovo?" I ask, to make sure this is the right train.

No reply.

The three look so picturesque in the costumes, I wish they'd allow me to take a photo, but they've made it clear they don't want to communicate.

I gaze out the window, a dusty pane between threadbare, red-dotted curtains. Pine-wooded slopes, deep green and black, rise steeply. The train labours uphill, chuffing and panting.

The grandmother seems to stare at me, yet when I turn to her and smile, I find the glassy-blue gaze of her eyes unfocused, empty, as if looking at nothing at all.

I try once more to break the silence. "Az sum avstraliika." My words ring out into the silence.

Persevering with courteous cheerfulness, I bend to pick up a bloom that's lying at the grandmother's leather-shoed feet. "I think this has fallen from your basket." I hold it out to her, but she makes no move to take it.

I grope for words which might fit the occasion. "Tsvetia. Rosa. Hubava." *Flowers. Rose. Lovely.* At least, I think that's what they mean.

No response.

My scalp itches, and the small hairs on the backs of my arms rise. I feel distinctly unwelcome and out of place.

I study the flower, a small bloom dense with reddish-pink petals. Its sweet scent reaches my nostrils, and I wonder if this is a damask rose, the source of Bulgaria's famed rose oil. But there's no point asking. The ladies have made it clear that they don't deem me worth noticing.

At the far end of the carriage sits a grim man with an oversized moustache, his dark-booted legs spread open. He looks like a

Turkish villain from the concrete bas-reliefs, only more colourful in a cobalt-blue Ottoman uniform with a black-tasselled, scarlet tarbush on his head. On his lap he holds... wait, is that an actual scimitar sword?

Maybe he's travelling to participate in some kind of reenactment event. Still, a man with an unsheathed blade, that's taking authenticity too far. My heart accelerates, pulses in my throat. I must be mistaken.

Before I can be sure of what I see, the train whooshes into a tunnel, and blackness fills the carriage.

Even though the air conditioning in this train functions, the lighting doesn't. Darkness suffuses everything.

Chuff-chuff, chuff-chuff the engine pants. *Ratatat ratatat* the wheels reply from below.

The thick smell of coal smoke wafts through an open window, but at the same time, the stink in the carriage intensifies. In the darkness, I can only guess that it originates from the women who may not have bathed for some time. Few village houses have bathrooms. Outhouses, and perhaps a hosepipe fed from a well pump, are the norm.

I hold the rose under my nose and inhale its sweet scent.

A few seconds pass, and daylight returns. Or rather, what is left of the day. Twilight.

The putrefying smell now almost makes me gag. Something is wrong here. Very wrong.

I hope we get to Dolno Orehovo soon. Surely any moment now we must roll into that station. I click my smartphone open to check. But there's no reception.

I stuff the phone and the rose into my backpack's side pocket, ready to leave as soon as the station comes into sight. I can't wait to get out of this creepy train.

Hoisting my backpack, I say "Dovishdaneh." *Goodbye.*

The grandmother's face has changed. It is white, with glassy staring eyes, and beneath it, a band of dripping scarlet circles her throat. Rivulets of red blood run down her front, stain the pristine white blouse, and drip into her flower basket saturating the petals of damask rose.

The sleeping girl has a red-rimmed gash in her throat, like a giant lipsticked grinning mouth.

The mother's decapitated head nestles on the crochet work in her lap.

Sickness and fear spiral from my stomach into my chest. I leap up to flee. I have to get out of here.

The Ottoman soldier with the cobalt-blue uniform, scimitar in hand, blocks my way. Under the dark moustache, he bares glistening teeth. Bright blood dripping from his sword matches the scarlet of his tarbush.

I try to scream, but the sound stays stuck in my throat.

Somehow I must get out.

Shutting my eyes and my consciousness to all I see, I focus my mind on the exit behind him.

I muster my strength, push past the soldier, and run.

I rip the door open, make it to the metal platform. Without pause or thought, I launch myself off the moving train.

I fall, roll, drop further. My head hits something hard. Black and yellow pain explodes in my skull.

*

I wake to the sound of snores and rattling trolley wheels.

When I try to sit up, a wave of sickness rises to my throat, and my head spins. I manage to heave myself into a half-seated position to view where I am: in a hospital, obviously. More specifically in a crowded ward, with over a dozen beds crammed so close together that if I wanted, I could reach and touch my neighbour's mattresses.

Grey-uniformed nurses bustle briskly past, not even responding to requests from patients.

A huge analog clock on the wall opposite gives the time: 6.03. Morning or evening? How long have I been here? Next to it, a plastic-framed print celebrates Bulgaria's most revered hero, Vasil Levski, in valiant blond masculinity.

A harried-looking doctor appears at my bedside, a plastic clipboard in her left hand, a ballpoint pen in the right. "You're awake. Good."

She rattles off a series of questions: "What's your name? Where do you live? What's your profession? Where are you staying? What year is it?"

I need to dig for the memory to give the answers she obviously already knows from documents they've found in my backpack. I'm a teacher in Melbourne. I teach Year 10 students, French and Art. With every reply, she ticks off a box, her pen scratching on the paper.

Finally I manage to ask my own question. "What happened? Why am I here?"

"You had an accident. A farmer found you unconscious by a roadside near a mountain village and called an ambulance. They brought you here." She glances at her watch. "The CAT scan has already been done. There's no lasting damage to your head. Just concussion. And your brain is obviously fully functioning. So you can return to your hotel. There's no need for you to stay."

"But..." I protest. "I felt nauseous when I woke up. And there's this pressure in my head."

"These are normal concussion symptoms. They'll pass. Just rest." She sighs at the sight of yet another bed being wheeled into the already crowded ward. "You'll be more comfortable in your hotel room."

All around, snores, wheezes and urgent beeps underscore what she says.

I'm sure she's right. But... "Why is my foot bandaged? And this pain in my side?"

The doctor rolls her eyes. "Just a sprained ankle and a cracked rib. Nothing dangerous. Don't put your full weight on the foot for a couple of days, but start walking as soon as you can bear the pain. And rest. Just rest." She heaves another sigh, this time so loud that I get the message: she envies me my leisure.

I agree to be discharged, and to come for a follow-up check as an outpatient in three days. Then my glance falls on the picture on the opposite wall again. Vasil Levski was the leader of Bulgaria's struggle against the Turks.

The Turks. The revolution. The massacres. Memories pound against my skull and demand answers.

What accident? How did I come to lie unconscious by the roadside?

"Just a moment, doctor. I have a question." Now what is it I want to ask? My head is spinning. "Do you have steam trains here in Bulgaria?"

The doctor frowns. "Steam trains? Not in service. There are some in museums, of course."

A chill wraps around my spine. "Then they were ghosts. The women with the roses. The Turk with the scimitar. It was a ghost train. And when I jumped off, I got hurt."

"Ghosts?" The doctor snaps to alertness. "Perhaps we need to keep you here for observation. There may be complications in your brain, something the scan hasn't detected.... " Her voice takes on a studied calm. "Tell me everything you remember about that day. Start with breakfast."

I recall my strenuous walks through mountain villages, the historical research for my blog, the visits to monasteries and revolutionary monuments, the museums dedicated to the massacre. I mention the unhelpfulness of the locals, the heat, the thirst and the tiredness, and how close I'd come to actually walking along the tracks when finally the train came.

Her face relaxes. "That's all right then, nothing to worry about. You hallucinated before your accident, not after. Heat exhaustion and dehydration can do that. The hallucinations made you fall. Your brain is perfectly well. We don't need to keep you here."

"I didn't hallucinate!" I protest. "This was real! I was there in that train. I saw the slaughter, I smelled it…"

She gives me a patronising, pitying smile. "You were exhausted, dehydrated, had a heat stroke. When you were stuck and no train came, you obviously decided to walk along the tracks all the way to Dolno Orehovo, poor thing."

"But I didn't walk to Dolno Orehovo. No way would I have…"

"You did. You were found shortly before Dolno Orehevo, at the bottom of a railway embankment. You'd obviously got disoriented, staggered, lost your footing – that's quite common with a heat stroke. And in addition, you had terrifying hallucinations about ghosts with scimitars. So you tumbled down the embankment and hit your head on a rock."

She assures me once more that the hallucinations were the result of heat exhaustion and dehydration, not of brain damage. Therefore, they are not her hospital's responsibility, and I need to vacate the hospital bed.

Viewed rationally, the explanation makes sense. In my despair, I really must have decided on the crazy plan to walk to Dolno

Orehovo, and on the way, exhausted by the day's strain, my fevered brain must have conjured up the ghost train.

Well, I'm glad I don't have any brain damage. And I'll really be more comfortable in the privacy of my hotel room. I promise willingly to refrain from strenuous walks and excessive heat for the rest of my holidays, and will instead laze by the hotel pool and sip cool drinks. I'll even pamper myself with a massage and a pedicure to celebrate that I'm perfectly sane.

I have to sign a dozen papers – all in Bulgarian and way beyond my comprehension. Supposedly they confirm that I consent to my health insurance covering the cost of the treatment, and that I agree to the discharge. Further signatures are required for the loan of a crutch, and a harried receptionist applies several stamps to each sheet.

I hoist my backpack, shut out the pain in my ankle as best I can, and hobble to the elevator.

*

Back at the hotel, I dump my backpack on the rug and my backside on the bed. The air conditioner whirrs, and delivers a cool caressing breeze. I'm safe.

For the rest of my holiday here, I'll rest my legs just like the doctor ordered, and sip iced water. No more walking tours, no more grumpy grandmas, no more crowded hospital wards. No more massacres, no more ghostly hallucinations. What a crazy nightmare mirage that had been, getting caught up in a 120-year-old massacre. If that's what dehydration and heat exhaustion do to you, I won't risk it ever again.

Now I need to check my texts and connect with the real world again. I rummage through my backpack. Ah, here's the phone, in the side pocket. My fingers meet something else... a hard, smooth knob, unfamiliar. I pull it out into the light.

It's a half-open rosebud, its pink petals faded at the edges, its stump of a stem gone limp.

My skin crawls. This is the rose I picked up from the carriage floor. If I didn't travel on that train, where did the rose come from?

The air fills with the cloying perfume of the decaying bloom.

DEAR READER,

I hope you enjoyed this visit to the romantic-creepy world of Gothic Fiction, and have gained ideas and inspiration for your own Gothic tales.

I'd love it if you could post a review on Amazon or some other book site where you have an account and posting privileges. Maybe you can mention what kind of fiction you write (or want to write), and which chapters you find most helpful and inspiring.

Email me the link to your review, and I'll send you a free review copy (ebook) of one of my other Writer's Craft books. Let me know which one you would like: *Writing Fight Scenes, Writing Scary Scenes, The Word-Loss Diet, Writing About Magic, Writing About Villains, Writing Dark Stories, Euphonics For Writers, Writing Short Stories to Promote Your Novels, Twitter for Writers, Why Does My Book Not Sell? 20 Simple Fixes, Writing Vivid Settings, How To Train Your Cat To Promote Your Book, Writing Deep Point of View, Getting Book Reviews, Novel Revision Prompts, Writing Vivid Dialogue, Writing Vivid Characters, Writing Book Blurbs and Synopses, Writing Vivid Plots, Write Your Way Out of Depression: Practical Self-Therapy For Creative Writers, Fantasy Writing Prompts, Horror Writing Prompts, How to Write That Scene, More Horror Writing Prompts, Writing Love Scenes, Author Branding, Ghostwriting....* (For a title list with brief descriptions, see this page on my website: https://www.raynehall.com/books-for-writers.)

My email is contact@raynehall.com. Drop me a line if you've spotted any typos which have escaped the proofreader's eagle eyes, want to give me private feedback or have questions.

You can also contact me on Twitter: https://twitter.com/RayneHall. Tweet me that you've read this book, and I'll probably follow you back.

If you find this book helpful, it would be great if you could spread the word about it. Maybe you know other writers who would benefit.

At the end of this book, you'll find an excerpt from another Writer's Craft Guide you may find useful, especially if you create Gothic Fiction. *Writing Vivid Emotions.* Enjoy!

With best wishes for your Gothic writing,

Rayne Hall

ACKNOWLEDGEMENTS

Sincere thanks to the critiquers and beta-readers who helped improve the draft chapters and gave valuable feedback on the completed manuscript: Anna Erishkigal, RG Austin, Natalia Prats, Linda Farmer Harris, Keira Morgan, Lisa Lawler, Robert Coleman, Kris Loomis, Douglas Kolacki, Phillip Stephens, Melissa Tacket. Thanks also to the members of the online group Professional Authors who participated in my original workshop on which I've based this guide: April Grey, Kate Casper, Chris Butcher, Mark Cassell and others.

The book cover is by Erica Syverson and Manuel Berbin. Katherine Pomeroy-Casper proofread the manuscript, and Eled Cernik formatted the book.

CHAPTER 6: DESCRIPTIONS CONVEY MOOD

In this chapter, I'll show you how you can subtly convey how the PoV character feels, and at the same time manipulate the reader's emotions.

When you describe something, use words that evoke emotional connotations. Focus especially on verbs.

Here are several sentences describing dusk. Each reflects a different emotion in the PoV and evokes a different mood in the reader.

Sunset gilded the horizon.

The sky bruised into night.

The sun dropped, taking the last remaining warmth with it.

The horizon throbbed crimson, then gentled to a soft pink.

Thick clouds hung on the horizon, and only a watery strip of orange peeked through.

The sun set, leaving a red-gashing wound between the earth and the sky.

The sky was sliding into dour night.

The day was already dying. Dusk hung like a purple mist.

The clouds at the horizon darkened. A sliver of the sinking sun glinted in their folds.

Sundown bloodied the horizon.

The sky flared up in hues of crimson and purple.

The last sliver of sunlight vanished from the sky.

Darkness came down like a hood.

The sun sank to rest behind the wagon track.

Within minutes, the fierce colours faded to pale.

Wind-ruffled pink clouds drifted along the horizon.

The sun slipped behind the dunes and cast a golden veil across their shifting shapes.

The sun painted a last, brilliant orange streak across the jagged mountain.

The sun died in streaks of gold and purple.

As you can see, there are many ways to describe a sunset. Obviously, not every one of these would suit every story and every writing style.

I've already used some of these in my novels, so if you want a sunset, don't copy my phrases but create your own mood-rich descriptions.

Here's another example. The PoV character sees another person who wears a gold choker around her neck.

Instead of simply stating

She wore a gold choker around her neck.

Try to convey how the PoV character feels about this woman, about the necklace, or about the situation in general. You might choose one of these:

A gold choker clawed at her neck.

A gold choker embraced her neck.

A gold choker caressed her neck.

A gold choker glinted around her neck.

A gold choker slithered around her neck.

A gold choker sparkled around her neck.

A gold choker snaked around her neck.

To convey or create positive emotions such as joy, hope and happiness, use positive verbs like *sparkle, dance, lap, skip, embrace, hug, shine, bloom, crown, caress.*

For dark moods and emotions, use verbs with negative connotations, such as *slash, rob, claw, stab, stump, steal, slither, scratch, dump, boil, scrape, squash, struggle, beg, clutch, grasp, devour, squeeze.*

EXAMPLE FROM LITERATURE

The Gabriel Hounds, Mary Stewart

When he had gone, I sat down on the divan cushions, looking out over the gorge where the last of the light netted the tips of the trees with gold. Below, the shadows deepened through purple to black. It would soon be dark.

WHAT NOT TO DO

Don't use in-your-face metaphors for descriptions. If the PoV character feels depressed, don't show heavy clouds in the sky. If she's desperate, don't show starving children in ragged clothes, and if she's happy, don't show a field of frolicking lambs. The effect would be melodramatic. Although melodrama has its uses in some kinds of fiction, most novels are better without it.

Beginners are prone to this mistake, especially when describing the weather. In novice-written stories it always rains when the character feels sad, and when she feels cheerful, the sun shines. In literary criticism, this is called a 'pathetic fallacy'.

For a subtler effect without melodrama, choose weather conditions, landscapes and objects which don't reflect the emotion – but evoke the mood through your word choices.

Your happy character may see ragged children on a litter-strewn pavement, and you can describe this in a positive way by using words like *play, fun, laugh, dance, skip.* An unhappy character may see a garden arch covered in roses, and through her filter of experience, it's a depressing sight if you use words like *smother, cling, snake, droop.*

PROFESSIONAL TIP

Use descriptions conveying emotions to foreshadow future plot events and to hint at things you don't spell out.

Perhaps it's evening, and one of the characters says she has to go home to her husband. She says it in a subdued voice, and her eyes have lost their sparkle. The readers understand that this woman doesn't look forward to spending the evening with that man, but don't know what's wrong. If you now insert a description of the sunset – *The sky bruised into night* – the readers will grasp on a subconscious level that the husband is a brutal man whose violence she fears.

If you choose to try this professional-level technique in your fiction, apply it with a light brush, so that readers are not consciously aware of what you are doing.

ASSIGNMENTS

1. Does your work-in-progress (WiP) have a scene which takes place in the evening? Consider how the PoV character feels. Write a sentence describing the sunset (or dusk, lights-out, descending darkness or other evening feature) with words that convey his emotions. Use the list of examples in this chapter as inspiration, without copying them. If your WiP has no evening scene at all, write about sunrise or high noon instead.

2. In a scene you are planning or revising, identify the PoV character's main emotion. Now consider the time of the day, the weather, and visualise the surroundings. How do they look, viewed through the filter of how the PoV character feels?

Printed in Poland
by Amazon Fulfillment
Poland Sp. z o.o., Wrocław

81596712R00106